Presented to

_____

by

_____

date

_____

God's
Promises®
for
Fathers

COUNTRYMAN®

A division of Thomas Nelson Publishers
Since 1798

Contents

GOD FREELY
GIVES YOU . . .

Eternal hope for your family

Sing to the LORD with thanksgiving;
Sing praises on the harp to our God,
Who covers the heavens with clouds,
Who prepares rain for the earth,
Who makes grass to grow on the mountains.
He gives to the beast its food,
And to the young ravens that cry.
He does not delight in the strength of the horse;
He takes no pleasure in the legs of a man.
The LORD takes pleasure in those who fear Him,
In those who hope in His mercy.
Praise the LORD, O Jerusalem!
Praise your God, O Zion!
For He has strengthened the bars of your gates;
He has blessed your children within you.

Psalm 147:7–13

For the wages of sin is death, but the gift of God is eternal life in Christ Jesus our Lord.

Romans 6:23

But let us who are of the day be sober, putting on the breastplate of faith and love, and as a helmet the hope of salvation. For God did not appoint us to wrath, but to obtain salvation through our Lord Jesus Christ, who died for us, that whether we wake or sleep, we should live together with Him.

Therefore comfort each other and edify one another, just as you also are doing.

1 Thessalonians 5:8–11

But God, who is rich in mercy, because of His great love with which He loved us, even when we were dead in trespasses, made us alive together with Christ (by grace you have been saved), and raised us up together, and made us sit together in the heavenly places in Christ Jesus, that in the ages to come He might show the exceeding riches of His grace in His kindness toward us in Christ Jesus.

Ephesians 2:4–7

If then you were raised with Christ, seek those things which are above, where Christ is, sitting at the right hand of God. Set your mind on things above, not on things on the earth. For you died, and your life is hidden with Christ in God. When Christ who is our life appears, then you also will appear with Him in glory.

Colossians 3:1–4

Because of the hope which is laid up for you in heaven, of which you heard before in the word of the truth of the gospel, which has come to you, as it has also in all the world, and is bringing forth fruit, as it is also among you since the day you heard and knew the grace of God in truth.

Colossians 1:5–6

Knowing that a man is not justified by the works of the law but by faith in Jesus Christ, even we have believed in Christ Jesus, that we might be justified by faith in Christ and not by the works of the law; for by the works of the law no flesh shall be justified. . . .

I have been crucified with Christ; it is no longer I who live, but Christ lives in me; and the life which I now live in the flesh I live by faith in the Son of God, who loved me and gave Himself for me.

Galatians 2:16, 20

Therefore let that abide in you which you heard from the beginning. If what you heard from the beginning abides in you, you also will abide in the Son and in the Father. And this is the promise that He has promised us—eternal life.

1 John 2:24–25

For as many as are led by the Spirit of God, these are sons of God. For you did not receive the spirit of bondage again to fear, but you received the Spirit of adoption by whom we cry out, "Abba, Father." The Spirit Himself bears witness with our spirit that we are children of God, and if children, then heirs—heirs of God and joint heirs with Christ, if indeed we suffer with Him, that we may also be glorified together.

For I consider that the sufferings of this present time are not worthy to be compared with the glory which shall be revealed in us. . . . For we were saved in this hope, but hope that is seen is not hope; for why does one still hope for what he sees? But if we hope for what we do not see, we eagerly wait for it with perseverance.

Romans 8:14–18, 24–25

I have fought the good fight, I have finished the race, I have kept the faith. Finally, there is laid up for me the crown of righteousness, which the Lord, the righteous Judge, will give to me on that Day, and not to me only but also to all who have loved His appearing.

2 Timothy 4:7–8

Blessed be the God and Father of our Lord Jesus Christ, who according to His abundant mercy has begotten us again to a living hope through the resurrection of Jesus Christ from the dead, to an inheritance incorruptible and undefiled and that does not fade away, reserved in heaven for you, who are kept by the power of God through faith for salvation ready to be revealed in the last time. In this you greatly rejoice, though now for a little while, if need be, you have been grieved by various trials, that the genuineness of your faith, being much more precious than gold that perishes, though it is tested by fire, may be found to praise, honor, and glory at the revelation of Jesus Christ, whom having not seen you love. Though now you do not see Him, yet believing, you rejoice with joy inexpressible and full of glory, receiving the end of your faith—the salvation of your souls.

1 Peter 1:3–9

The wisdom you seek
for your children

My son, pay attention to my wisdom;
    Lend your ear to my understanding,
That you may preserve discretion,
    And your lips may keep knowledge.

Proverbs 5:1–2

The fear of the LORD is the beginning of wisdom;
    A good understanding have all those who do
        His commandments.
    His praise endures forever.

Psalm 111:10

The days of our lives are seventy years;
    And if by reason of strength they are eighty years,
    Yet their boast is only labor and sorrow;
    For it is soon cut off, and we fly away.
Who knows the power of Your anger?
    For as the fear of You, so is Your wrath.
So teach us to number our days,
    That we may gain a heart of wisdom.

Psalm 90:10–12

Oh, how I love Your law!
  It is my meditation all the day.
You, through Your commandments, make me
    wiser than my enemies;
  For they are ever with me.
I have more understanding than all my teachers,
  For Your testimonies are my meditation.
I understand more than the ancients,
  Because I keep Your precepts.
I have restrained my feet from every evil way,
  That I may keep Your word.
I have not departed from Your judgments,
  For You Yourself have taught me.
How sweet are Your words to my taste,
  Sweeter than honey to my mouth!
Through Your precepts I get understanding;
  Therefore I hate every false way.

Psalm 119:97–104

How much better to get wisdom than gold!
  And to get understanding is to be chosen
    rather than silver.

Proverbs 16:16

"Get wisdom! Get understanding!
  Do not forget, nor turn away from the words
    of my mouth.
Do not forsake her, and she will preserve you;
  Love her, and she will keep you.
Wisdom is the principal thing;
  Therefore get wisdom. And in all your getting,
    get understanding.
Exalt her, and she will promote you;
  She will bring you honor, when you embrace her.
She will place on your head an ornament
    of grace;
  A crown of glory she will deliver to you."
Hear, my son, and receive my sayings,
  And the years of your life will be many.
I have taught you in the way of wisdom;
  I have led you in right paths.

Proverbs 4:5–11

But the wisdom that is from above is first pure,
then peaceable, gentle, willing to yield, full of mercy
and good fruits, without partiality and without hypocrisy.

James 3:17

Happy is the man who finds wisdom,
    And the man who gains understanding;
For her proceeds are better than the profits of silver,
    And her gain than fine gold.
She is more precious than rubies,
    And all the things you may desire cannot
        compare with her.
Length of days is in her right hand,
    In her left hand riches and honor.
Her ways are ways of pleasantness,
    And all her paths are peace.
She is a tree of life to those who take hold of her,
    And happy are all who retain her.
The LORD by wisdom founded the earth;
    By understanding He established the heavens;
By His knowledge the depths were broken up,
    And clouds drop down the dew.
My son, let them not depart from your eyes—
    Keep sound wisdom and discretion;
So they will be life to your soul
    And grace to your neck.

Proverbs 3:13–22

However, we speak wisdom among those who are mature, yet not the wisdom of this age, nor of the rulers of this age, who are coming to nothing. But we speak the wisdom of God in a mystery, the hidden wisdom which God ordained before the ages for our glory, which none of the rulers of this age knew; for had they known, they would not have crucified the Lord of glory.

But as it is written:

"Eye has not seen, nor ear heard,
Nor have entered into the heart of man
The things which God has prepared for those
   who love Him."

1 Corinthians 2:6–9

If any of you lacks wisdom, let him ask of God, who gives to all liberally and without reproach, and it will be given to him. But let him ask in faith, with no doubting, for he who doubts is like a wave of the sea driven and tossed by the wind.

James 1:5–6

His peace in troubled times

The LORD builds up Jerusalem;
    He gathers together the outcasts of Israel.
He heals the brokenhearted
    And binds up their wounds. . . .
Great is our Lord, and mighty in power;
    His understanding is infinite.
The LORD lifts up the humble;
    He casts the wicked down to the ground. . . .
For He has strengthened the bars of your gates;
    He has blessed your children within you.
He makes peace in your borders,
    And fills you with the finest wheat.

Psalm 147:2–3, 5–6, 13–14

Turn Yourself to me, and have mercy on me,
    For I am desolate and afflicted.
The troubles of my heart have enlarged;
    Bring me out of my distresses!
Look on my affliction and my pain,
    And forgive all my sins.

Psalm 25:16–18

A horse is a vain hope for safety;

    Neither shall it deliver any by its great strength.

Behold, the eye of the LORD is on those who

      fear Him,

    On those who hope in His mercy,

To deliver their soul from death,

    And to keep them alive in famine.

Our soul waits for the LORD;

    He is our help and our shield.

For our heart shall rejoice in Him,

    Because we have trusted in His holy name.

Let Your mercy, O LORD, be upon us,

    Just as we hope in You.

Psalm 33:17–22

Casting all your care upon Him, for He cares for you. Be sober, be vigilant; because your adversary the devil walks about like a roaring lion, seeking whom he may devour. Resist him, steadfast in the faith, knowing that the same sufferings are experienced by your brotherhood in the world. But may the God of all grace, who called us to His eternal glory by Christ Jesus, after you have suffered a while, perfect, establish, strengthen, and settle you. To Him be the glory and the dominion forever and ever. Amen.

1 Peter 5:7–11

I will bless the LORD at all times;
  His praise shall continually be in my mouth.
My soul shall make its boast in the LORD;
  The humble shall hear of it and be glad.
Oh, magnify the LORD with me,
  And let us exalt His name together.
I sought the LORD, and He heard me,
  And delivered me from all my fears.
They looked to Him and were radiant,
  And their faces were not ashamed.
This poor man cried out, and the LORD heard him,
  And saved him out of all his troubles.
The angel of the LORD encamps all around those
    who fear Him,
  And delivers them.
Oh, taste and see that the LORD is good;
  Blessed is the man who trusts in Him!

Psalm 34:1–8

"Peace I leave with you, My peace I give to you; not as the world gives do I give to you. Let not your heart be troubled, neither let it be afraid."

John 14:27

You are of God, little children, and have overcome them, because He who is in you is greater than he who is in the world.

1 John 4:4

I will be glad and rejoice in Your mercy,
   For You have considered my trouble;
   You have known my soul in adversities.

Psalm 31:7

Victory over the sins in your life

—❦—

Therefore, if anyone is in Christ, he is a new creation; old things have passed away; behold, all things have become new. Now all things are of God, who has reconciled us to Himself through Jesus Christ, and has given us the ministry of reconciliation, that is, that God was in Christ reconciling the world to Himself, not imputing their trespasses to them, and has committed to us the word of reconciliation. Now then, we are ambassadors for Christ, as though God were pleading through us: we implore you on Christ's behalf, be reconciled to God. For He made Him who knew no sin to be sin for us, that we might become the righteousness of God in Him.

2 Corinthians 5:17–21

For as many as are of the works of the law are under the curse; for it is written, "Cursed is everyone who does not continue in all things which are written in the book of the law, to do them."

But that no one is justified by the law in the sight of God is evident, for "the just shall live by faith."

Galatians 3:10–11

O God, You know my foolishness;
  And my sins are not hidden from You.

Psalm 69:5

"Wash yourselves, make yourselves clean;
  Put away the evil of your doings from before
    My eyes.
  Cease to do evil,
Learn to do good;
  Seek justice,
  Rebuke the oppressor;
  Defend the fatherless,
  Plead for the widow.
Come now, and let us reason together,"
  Says the LORD,
"Though your sins are like scarlet,
  They shall be as white as snow;
  Though they are red like crimson,
They shall be as wool.
If you are willing and obedient,
  You shall eat the good of the land."

Isaiah 1:16–19

Stand fast therefore in the liberty by which Christ has made us free, and do not be entangled again with a yoke of bondage.

Galatians 5:1

Therefore, since we have this ministry, as we have received mercy, we do not lose heart. But we have renounced the hidden things of shame, not walking in craftiness nor handling the word of God deceitfully, but by manifestation of the truth commending ourselves to every man's conscience in the sight of God. But even if our gospel is veiled, it is veiled to those who are perishing, whose minds the god of this age has blinded, who do not believe, lest the light of the gospel of the glory of Christ, who is the image of God, should shine on them. For we do not preach ourselves, but Christ Jesus the Lord, and ourselves your bondservants for Jesus' sake. For it is the God who commanded light to shine out of darkness, who has shone in our hearts to give the light of the knowledge of the glory of God in the face of Jesus Christ.

2 Corinthians 4:1–6

"O Death, where is your sting?
O Hades, where is your victory?"
The sting of death is sin, and the strength of sin is the law. But thanks be to God, who gives us the victory through our Lord Jesus Christ.

Therefore, my beloved brethren, be steadfast, immovable, always abounding in the work of the Lord, knowing that your labor is not in vain in the Lord.

1 Corinthians 15:55–58

Finally, my brethren, be strong in the Lord and in the power of His might. Put on the whole armor of God, that you may be able to stand against the wiles of the devil. For we do not wrestle against flesh and blood, but against principalities, against powers, against the rulers of the darkness of this age, against spiritual hosts of wickedness in the heavenly places. Therefore take up the whole armor of God, that you may be able to withstand in the evil day, and having done all, to stand.

Stand therefore, having girded your waist with truth, having put on the breastplate of righteousness, and having shod your feet with the preparation of the gospel of peace; above all, taking the shield of faith with which you will be able to quench all the fiery darts of the wicked one. And take the helmet of salvation, and the sword of the Spirit, which is the word of God; praying always with all prayer and supplication in the Spirit, being watchful to this end with all perseverance and supplication for all the saints.

Ephesians 6:10–18

This is the message which we have heard from Him and declare to you, that God is light and in Him is no darkness at all. If we say that we have fellowship with Him, and walk in darkness, we lie and do not practice the truth. But if we walk in the light as He is in the light, we have fellowship with one another, and the blood of Jesus Christ His Son cleanses us from all sin. If we say that we have no sin, we deceive ourselves, and the truth is not in us. If we confess our sins, He is faithful and just to forgive us our sins and to cleanse us from all unrighteousness. If we say that we have not sinned, we make Him a liar, and His word is not in us.

1 John 1:5–10

Power to defeat
your deepest fears

And God heard the voice of the lad. Then the angel of God called to Hagar out of heaven, and said to her, "What ails you, Hagar? Fear not, for God has heard the voice of the lad where he is. Arise, lift up the lad and hold him with your hand, for I will make him a great nation."

Then God opened her eyes, and she saw a well of water. And she went and filled the skin with water, and gave the lad a drink. So God was with the lad; and he grew and dwelt in the wilderness, and became an archer.

Genesis 21:17–20

Yet in all these things we are more than conquerors through Him who loved us. For I am persuaded that neither death nor life, nor angels nor principalities nor powers, nor things present nor things to come, nor height nor depth, nor any other created thing, shall be able to separate us from the love of God which is in Christ Jesus our Lord.

Romans 8:37–39

Oh, magnify the LORD with me,
  And let us exalt His name together.
I sought the LORD, and He heard me,
  And delivered me from all my fears.
They looked to Him and were radiant,
  And their faces were not ashamed.
This poor man cried out, and the LORD heard him,
  And saved him out of all his troubles.
The angel of the LORD encamps all around those
    who fear Him,
  And delivers them.
Oh, taste and see that the LORD is good;
  Blessed is the man who trusts in Him!

Psalm 34:3–8

But Joshua the son of Nun and Caleb the son of Jephunneh, who were among those who had spied out the land, tore their clothes; and they spoke to all the congregation of the children of Israel, saying: "The land we passed through to spy out is an exceedingly good land. If the LORD delights in us, then He will bring us into this land and give it to us, 'a land which flows with milk and honey.' Only do not rebel against the LORD, nor fear the people of the land, for they are our bread; their protection has departed from them, and the LORD is with us. Do not fear them."

Numbers 14:6–9

"Look, the LORD your God has set the land before you; go up and possess it, as the LORD God of your fathers has spoken to you; do not fear or be discouraged."

And every one of you came near to me and said, "Let us send men before us, and let them search out the land for us, and bring back word to us of the way by which we should go up, and of the cities into which we shall come."

The plan pleased me well; so I took twelve of your men, one man from each tribe. And they departed and went up into the mountains, and came to the Valley of Eshcol, and spied it out. They also took some of the fruit of the land in their hands and brought it down to us; and they brought back word to us, saying, "It is a good land which the LORD our God is giving us."

Nevertheless you would not go up, but rebelled against the command of the LORD your God; and you complained in your tents, and said, "Because the LORD hates us, He has brought us out of the land of Egypt to deliver us into the hand of the Amorites, to destroy us.

Where can we go up? Our brethren have discouraged our hearts, saying, 'The people are greater and taller than we; the cities are great and fortified up to heaven; moreover we have seen the sons of the Anakim there.'"

Then I said to you, "Do not be terrified, or afraid of them. The LORD your God, who goes before you, He will fight for you, according to all He did for you in Egypt before your eyes, and in the wilderness where you saw how the LORD your God carried you, as a man carries his son, in all the way that you went until you came to this place."

Deuteronomy 1:21–31

Why should I fear in the days of evil,
　　When the iniquity at my heels surrounds me?
Those who trust in their wealth
　　And boast in the multitude of their riches. . . .
But God will redeem my soul from the power of
　　the grave,
　　For He shall receive me. Selah
Do not be afraid when one becomes rich,
　　When the glory of his house is increased;
For when he dies he shall carry nothing away;
　　His glory shall not descend after him.

Psalm 49:5–6, 15–17

Do not be afraid of sudden terror,
    Nor of trouble from the wicked when it comes;
For the LORD will be your confidence,
    And will keep your foot from being caught.

Proverbs 3:25–26

After these things the word of the LORD came to Abram in a vision, saying, "Do not be afraid, Abram. I am your shield, your exceedingly great reward."

Genesis 15:1

The courage to be a man of integrity

Blessed is the man
   Who walks not in the counsel of the ungodly,
   Nor stands in the path of sinners,
   Nor sits in the seat of the scornful;
But his delight is in the law of the LORD,
   And in His law he meditates day and night.
He shall be like a tree
   Planted by the rivers of water,
   That brings forth its fruit in its season,
   Whose leaf also shall not wither;
   And whatever he does shall prosper.
The ungodly are not so,
   But are like the chaff which the wind drives
      away.
Therefore the ungodly shall not stand in the
      judgment,
   Nor sinners in the congregation of the righteous.
For the LORD knows the way of the righteous,
   But the way of the ungodly shall perish.

Psalm 1:1–6

A good man deals graciously and lends;
    He will guide his affairs with discretion.
Surely he will never be shaken;
    The righteous will be in everlasting remembrance.
He will not be afraid of evil tidings;
    His heart is steadfast, trusting in the LORD.

Psalm 112:5–7

Blessed are the undefiled in the way,
    Who walk in the law of the LORD!
Blessed are those who keep His testimonies,
    Who seek Him with the whole heart!
They also do no iniquity;
    They walk in His ways.
You have commanded us
    To keep Your precepts diligently.
Oh, that my ways were directed
    To keep Your statutes!
Then I would not be ashamed,
    When I look into all Your commandments.
I will praise You with uprightness of heart,
    When I learn Your righteous judgments.
I will keep Your statutes;
    Oh, do not forsake me utterly!

Psalm 119:1–8

Then Phinehas stood up and intervened,
    And the plague was stopped.
And that was accounted to him for righteousness
    To all generations forevermore.

Psalm 106:30–31

Dishonest scales are an abomination to the Lord,
    But a just weight is His delight.
When pride comes, then comes shame;
    But with the humble is wisdom.
The integrity of the upright will guide them,
    But the perversity of the unfaithful will destroy
        them.

Proverbs 11:1–3

He who speaks truth declares righteousness,
    But a false witness, deceit.
There is one who speaks like the piercings of a sword,
    But the tongue of the wise promotes health.
The truthful lip shall be established forever,
    But a lying tongue is but for a moment.

Proverbs 12:17–19

Diverse weights are an abomination to the Lord,
    And dishonest scales are not good.

Proverbs 20:23

I will behave wisely in a perfect way.
Oh, when will You come to me?
I will walk within my house with a perfect
heart.
I will set nothing wicked before my eyes;
I hate the work of those who fall away;
It shall not cling to me.
A perverse heart shall depart from me;
I will not know wickedness.
Whoever secretly slanders his neighbor,
Him I will destroy;
The one who has a haughty look and a
proud heart,
Him I will not endure.
My eyes shall be on the faithful of the land,
That they may dwell with me;
He who walks in a perfect way,
He shall serve me.
He who works deceit shall not dwell within
my house;
He who tells lies shall not continue in my pres-
ence.
Early I will destroy all the wicked of the land,
That I may cut off all the evildoers from the
city of the LORD.

Psalm 101:2–8

The LORD shall judge the peoples;
    Judge me, O LORD, according to my
       righteousness,
    And according to my integrity within me.

Psalm 7:8

Let us draw near with a true heart in full assurance of faith, having our hearts sprinkled from an evil conscience and our bodies washed with pure water.

Hebrews 10:22

GOD ASKS
YOU TO . . .

Instruct your children
in His Word

Hear, my children, the instruction of a father,
    And give attention to know understanding;
For I give you good doctrine:
    Do not forsake my law.
When I was my father's son,
    Tender and the only one in the sight of my
        mother,
He also taught me, and said to me:
    "Let your heart retain my words;
    Keep my commands, and live."

Proverbs 4:1–4

My son, give attention to my words;
    Incline your ear to my sayings.
Do not let them depart from your eyes;
    Keep them in the midst of your heart;
For they are life to those who find them,
    And health to all their flesh.

Proverbs 4:20–22

Give ear, O my people, to my law;
  Incline your ears to the words of my mouth.
I will open my mouth in a parable;
  I will utter dark sayings of old,
Which we have heard and known,
  And our fathers have told us.
We will not hide them from their children,
  Telling to the generation to come the praises of
    the LORD,
  And His strength and His wonderful works
    that He has done.
For He established a testimony in Jacob,
  And appointed a law in Israel,
  Which He commanded our fathers,
  That they should make them known to their
    children;
That the generation to come might know them,
  The children who would be born,
  That they may arise and declare them to their
    children,
That they may set their hope in God,
  And not forget the works of God,
  But keep His commandments;
And may not be like their fathers,
  A stubborn and rebellious generation,
  A generation that did not set its heart aright,
  And whose spirit was not faithful to God.

Psalm 78:1–8

Now therefore, listen to me, my children,
For blessed are those who keep my ways.
Hear instruction and be wise,
And do not disdain it.
Blessed is the man who listens to me,
Watching daily at my gates,
Waiting at the posts of my doors.
For whoever finds me finds life,
And obtains favor from the LORD.

Proverbs 8:32–35

I do not write these things to shame you, but as my beloved children I warn you. For though you might have ten thousand instructors in Christ, yet you do not have many fathers; for in Christ Jesus I have begotten you through the gospel. Therefore I urge you, imitate me. For this reason I have sent Timothy to you, who is my beloved and faithful son in the Lord, who will remind you of my ways in Christ, as I teach everywhere in every church.

Now some are puffed up, as though I were not coming to you. But I will come to you shortly, if the Lord wills, and I will know, not the word of those who are puffed up, but the power. For the kingdom of God is not in word but in power. What do you want? Shall I come to you with a rod, or in love and a spirit of gentleness?

1 Corinthians 4:14–21

A wise man will hear and increase learning,
  And a man of understanding will attain wise
    counsel,
To understand a proverb and an enigma,
  The words of the wise and their riddles.
The fear of the LORD is the beginning of knowledge,
  But fools despise wisdom and instruction.
My son, hear the instruction of your father,
  And do not forsake the law of your mother;
For they will be a graceful ornament on your head,
  And chains about your neck.

Proverbs 1:5–9

All Scripture is given by inspiration of God, and is profitable for doctrine, for reproof, for correction, for instruction in righteousness.

2 Timothy 3:16

"All flesh is as grass,
And all the glory of man as the flower of the grass.
The grass withers,
And its flower falls away,
But the word of the LORD endures forever."
Now this is the word which by the gospel was preached to you.

1 Peter 1:24–25

For the word of God is living and powerful, and sharper than any two-edged sword, piercing even to the division of soul and spirit, and of joints and marrow, and is a discerner of the thoughts and intents of the heart.

Hebrews 4:12

But be doers of the word, and not hearers only, deceiving yourselves.

James 1:22

Therefore, laying aside all malice, all deceit, hypocrisy, envy, and all evil speaking, as newborn babes, desire the pure milk of the word, that you may grow thereby.

1 Peter 2:1–2

I will go in the strength of the Lord GOD;
    I will make mention of Your righteousness, of
        Yours only.
O God, You have taught me from my youth;
    And to this day I declare Your wondrous works.
Now also when I am old and grayheaded,
    O God, do not forsake me,
    Until I declare Your strength to this generation,
    Your power to everyone who is to come.

Psalm 71:16–18

Teach your children to pray

But will God indeed dwell on the earth? Behold, heaven and the heaven of heavens cannot contain You. How much less this temple which I have built! Yet regard the prayer of Your servant and his supplication, O LORD my God, and listen to the cry and the prayer which Your servant is praying before You today: that Your eyes may be open toward this temple night and day, toward the place of which You said, "My name shall be there," that You may hear the prayer which Your servant makes toward this place. And may You hear the supplication of Your servant and of Your people Israel, when they pray toward this place. Hear in heaven Your dwelling place; and when You hear, forgive.

1 Kings 8:27–30

And whatever we ask we receive from Him, because we keep His commandments and do those things that are pleasing in His sight.

1 John 3:22

"Therefore I say to you, whatever things you ask when you pray, believe that you receive them, and you will have them."

Mark 11:24

Call to Me, and I will answer you, and show you great and mighty things, which you do not know.

Jeremiah 33:3

For You, O LORD of hosts, God of Israel, have revealed this to Your servant, saying, "I will build you a house." Therefore Your servant has found it in his heart to pray this prayer to You.

And now, O Lord GOD, You are God, and Your words are true, and You have promised this goodness to Your servant.

2 Samuel 7:27–28

Let us therefore come boldly to the throne of grace, that we may obtain mercy and find grace to help in time of need.

Hebrews 4:16

It shall come to pass
That before they call, I will answer;
And while they are still speaking, I will hear.

Isaiah 65:24

For we were saved in this hope, but hope that is seen is not hope; for why does one still hope for what he sees? But if we hope for what we do not see, we eagerly wait for it with perseverance.

Likewise the Spirit also helps in our weaknesses. For we do not know what we should pray for as we ought, but the Spirit Himself makes intercession for us with groanings which cannot be uttered. Now He who searches the hearts knows what the mind of the Spirit is, because He makes intercession for the saints according to the will of God.

And we know that all things work together for good to those who love God, to those who are the called according to His purpose.

Romans 8:24–28

"And when you pray, you shall not be like the hypocrites. For they love to pray standing in the synagogues and on the corners of the streets, that they may be seen by men. Assuredly, I say to you, they have their reward. But you, when you pray, go into your room, and when you have shut your door, pray to your Father who is in the secret place; and your Father who sees in secret will reward you openly. And when you pray, do not use vain repetitions as the heathen do. For they think that they will be heard for their many words.

Therefore do not be like them. For your Father knows the things you have need of before you ask Him. In this manner, therefore, pray:

Our Father in heaven,
Hallowed be Your name.
Your kingdom come.
Your will be done
On earth as it is in heaven.
Give us this day our daily bread.
And forgive us our debts,
As we forgive our debtors.
And do not lead us into temptation,
But deliver us from the evil one.
For Yours is the kingdom and the power and the
glory forever. Amen."

Matthew 6:5–13

These things I have written to you who believe in the name of the Son of God, that you may know that you have eternal life, and that you may continue to believe in the name of the Son of God.

Now this is the confidence that we have in Him, that if we ask anything according to His will, He hears us. And if we know that He hears us, whatever we ask, we know that we have the petitions that we have asked of Him.

1 John 5:13–15

Reach out to families who are homeless

You shall rejoice before the LORD your God, you and your son and your daughter, your male servant and your female servant, the Levite who is within your gates, the stranger and the fatherless and the widow who are among you, at the place where the LORD your God chooses to make His name abide.

Deuteronomy 16:11

Yet they seek Me daily,
  And delight to know My ways,
  As a nation that did righteousness,
  And did not forsake the ordinance of their God.
  They ask of Me the ordinances of justice;
  They take delight in approaching God.

Isaiah 58:2

Let brotherly love continue. Do not forget to entertain strangers, for by so doing some have unwittingly entertained angels.

Hebrews 13:1–2

Is it not to share your bread with the hungry,
  And that you bring to your house the poor
      who are cast out;
  When you see the naked, that you cover him,
  And not hide yourself from your own flesh?
Then your light shall break forth like the morning,
  Your healing shall spring forth speedily,
  And your righteousness shall go before you;
  The glory of the LORD shall be your rear guard.
Then you shall call, and the LORD will answer;
  You shall cry, and He will say, "Here I am."
  If you take away the yoke from your midst,
  The pointing of the finger, and speaking
      wickedness,
If you extend your soul to the hungry
And satisfy the afflicted soul,
  Then your light shall dawn in the darkness,
  And your darkness shall be as the noonday.
  The LORD will guide you continually,
And satisfy your soul in drought,
  And strengthen your bones;
  You shall be like a watered garden,
  And like a spring of water, whose waters do
      not fail.

Isaiah 58:7–11

"Then the King will say to those on His right hand, 'Come, you blessed of My Father, inherit the kingdom prepared for you from the foundation of the world: for I was hungry and you gave Me food; I was thirsty and you gave Me drink; I was a stranger and you took Me in; I was naked and you clothed Me; I was sick and you visited Me; I was in prison and you came to Me.' Then the righteous will answer Him, saying, 'Lord, when did we see You hungry and feed You, or thirsty and give You drink? When did we see You a stranger and take You in, or naked and clothe You? Or when did we see You sick, or in prison, and come to You?' And the King will answer and say to them, 'Assuredly, I say to you, inasmuch as you did it to one of the least of these My brethren, you did it to Me.'"

Matthew 25:34–40

But whoever has this world's goods, and sees his brother in need, and shuts up his heart from him, how does the love of God abide in him?

My little children, let us not love in word or in tongue, but in deed and in truth. And by this we know that we are of the truth, and shall assure our hearts before Him.

1 John 3:17–19

Whoever shuts his ears to the cry of the poor
Will also cry himself and not be heard.

Proverbs 21:13

Happy is he who has the God of Jacob for
his help,
Whose hope is in the LORD his God,
Who made heaven and earth,
The sea, and all that is in them;
Who keeps truth forever,
Who executes justice for the oppressed,
Who gives food to the hungry.
The LORD gives freedom to the prisoners.
The LORD opens the eyes of the blind;
The LORD raises those who are bowed down;
The LORD loves the righteous.
The LORD watches over the strangers;
He relieves the fatherless and widow;
But the way of the wicked He turns upside
down.
The LORD shall reign forever—
Your God, O Zion, to all generations.
Praise the LORD!

Psalm 146:5–10

And above all things have fervent love for one another, for "love will cover a multitude of sins." Be hospitable to one another without grumbling. As each one has received a gift, minister it to one another, as good stewards of the manifold grace of God.

1 Peter 4:8–10

When you reap the harvest of your land, you shall not wholly reap the corners of your field, nor shall you gather the gleanings of your harvest. And you shall not glean your vineyard, nor shall you gather every grape of your vineyard; you shall leave them for the poor and the stranger: I am the LORD your God.

Leviticus 19:9–10

Love your neighbors

"You shall love your neighbor as yourself."
Matthew 19:19

Do not say to your neighbor,
  "Go, and come back,
  And tomorrow I will give it,"
  When you have it with you.
Do not devise evil against your neighbor,
  For he dwells by you for safety's sake.
Proverbs 3:28–29

He who despises his neighbor sins;
  But he who has mercy on the poor, happy is he.
Proverbs 14:21

He who is devoid of wisdom despises his neighbor,
  But a man of understanding holds his peace.
Proverbs 11:12

You shall not cheat your neighbor, nor rob him.
Leviticus 19:13

Do not go hastily to court;
   For what will you do in the end,
   When your neighbor has put you to shame?
Debate your case with your neighbor,
   And do not disclose the secret to another.

Proverbs 25:8–9

You shall not bear false witness against your neighbor.
   You shall not covet your neighbor's house; you shall
not covet your neighbor's wife, nor his male servant,
nor his female servant, nor his ox, nor his donkey, nor
anything that is your neighbor's.

Exodus 20:16–17

Whoever secretly slanders his neighbor,
   Him I will destroy;
   The one who has a haughty look and a proud
      heart,
   Him I will not endure.
My eyes shall be on the faithful of the land,
   That they may dwell with me;
   He who walks in a perfect way,
   He shall serve me.
He who works deceit shall not dwell within
      my house;
   He who tells lies shall not continue in my
      presence.

Psalm 101:5–7

But he, wanting to justify himself, said to Jesus, "And who is my neighbor?"

Then Jesus answered and said: "A certain man went down from Jerusalem to Jericho, and fell among thieves, who stripped him of his clothing, wounded him, and departed, leaving him half dead. Now by chance a certain priest came down that road. And when he saw him, he passed by on the other side. Likewise a Levite, when he arrived at the place, came and looked, and passed by on the other side. But a certain Samaritan, as he journeyed, came where he was. And when he saw him, he had compassion. So he went to him and bandaged his wounds, pouring on oil and wine; and he set him on his own animal, brought him to an inn, and took care of him. On the next day, when he departed, he took out two denarii, gave them to the innkeeper, and said to him, 'Take care of him; and whatever more you spend, when I come again, I will repay you.' So which of these three do you think was neighbor to him who fell among the thieves?"

And he said, "He who showed mercy on him."

Then Jesus said to him, "Go and do likewise."

Luke 10:29–37

And do not be conformed to this world, but be transformed by the renewing of your mind, that you may prove what is that good and acceptable and perfect will of God.

For I say, through the grace given to me, to every-one who is among you, not to think of himself more highly than he ought to think, but to think soberly, as God has dealt to each one a measure of faith.

Romans 12:2–3

Teach your children gratitude

—✧❦✧—

If indeed you have tasted that the Lord is gracious.
1 Peter 2:3

Now therefore, write down this song for your-selves, and teach it to the children of Israel; put it in their mouths, that this song may be a witness for Me against the children of Israel. When I have brought them to the land flowing with milk and honey, of which I swore to their fathers, and they have eaten and filled themselves and grown fat, then they will turn to other gods and serve them; and they will pro-voke Me and break My covenant. Then it shall be, when many evils and troubles have come upon them, that this song will testify against them as a witness; for it will not be forgotten in the mouths of their de-scendants, for I know the inclination of their behavior today, even before I have brought them to the land of which I swore to give them.

Deuteronomy 31:19–21

And my spirit has rejoiced in God my Savior.
Luke 1:47

Make a joyful shout to the LORD, all you lands!
Serve the LORD with gladness;
Come before His presence with singing.

Psalm 100:1–2

And that their children, who have not known it, may hear and learn to fear the LORD your God as long as you live in the land which you cross the Jordan to possess.

Deuteronomy 31:13

Finally, brethren, whatever things are true, whatever things are noble, whatever things are just, whatever things are pure, whatever things are lovely, whatever things are of good report, if there is any virtue and if there is anything praiseworthy—meditate on these things. The things which you learned and received and heard and saw in me, these do, and the God of peace will be with you.

But I rejoiced in the Lord greatly that now at last your care for me has flourished again; though you surely did care, but you lacked opportunity. Not that I speak in regard to need, for I have learned in whatever state I am, to be content.

Philippians 4:8–11

Sing praise to the Lord, you saints of His,
  And give thanks at the remembrance of His
    holy name.
For His anger is but for a moment,
  His favor is for life;
  Weeping may endure for a night,
  But joy comes in the morning.
Now in my prosperity I said,
  "I shall never be moved."

Psalm 30:4–6

But I determined this within myself, that I would not come again to you in sorrow. For if I make you sorrowful, then who is he who makes me glad but the one who is made sorrowful by me?

And I wrote this very thing to you, lest, when I came, I should have sorrow over those from whom I ought to have joy, having confidence in you all that my joy is the joy of you all.

2 Corinthians 2:1–3

Let your conduct be without covetousness; be content with such things as you have. For He Himself has said, "I will never leave you nor forsake you."

Hebrews 13:5

Now it happened as He went to Jerusalem that He passed through the midst of Samaria and Galilee. Then as He entered a certain village, there met Him ten men who were lepers, who stood afar off. And they lifted up their voices and said, "Jesus, Master, have mercy on us!"

So when He saw them, He said to them, "Go, show yourselves to the priests." And so it was that as they went, they were cleansed.

And one of them, when he saw that he was healed, returned, and with a loud voice glorified God, and fell down on his face at His feet, giving Him thanks. And he was a Samaritan.

So Jesus answered and said, "Were there not ten cleansed? But where are the nine? Were there not any found who returned to give glory to God except this foreigner?" And He said to him, "Arise, go your way. Your faith has made you well."

Luke 17:11–19

Show kindness to your family

———⟨⟩———

"Or what man is there among you who, if his son asks for bread, will give him a stone? Or if he asks for a fish, will he give him a serpent? If you then, being evil, know how to give good gifts to your children, how much more will your Father who is in heaven give good things to those who ask Him!"

Matthew 7:9–11

Then his father Isaac said to him, "Come near now and kiss me, my son."

Genesis 27:26

I traverse the way of righteousness,
    In the midst of the paths of justice,
That I may cause those who love me to
        inherit wealth,
    That I may fill their treasuries.
"The LORD possessed me at the beginning of
        His way,
    Before His works of old."

Proverbs 8:20–22

"Now therefore, I beg you, swear to me by the LORD, since I have shown you kindness, that you also will show kindness to my father's house, and give me a true token, and spare my father, my mother, my brothers, my sisters, and all that they have, and deliver our lives from death."

So the men answered her, "Our lives for yours, if none of you tell this business of ours. And it shall be, when the LORD has given us the land, that we will deal kindly and truly with you."

Joshua 2:12–14

Whoever has no rule over his own spirit
   Is like a city broken down, without walls.

Proverbs 25:28

"Yet it shall not be so among you; but whoever desires to become great among you shall be your servant. And whoever of you desires to be first shall be slave of all. For even the Son of Man did not come to be served, but to serve, and to give His life a ransom for many."

Mark 10:43–45

Do not be overcome by evil, but overcome evil with good.

Romans 12:21

Let all bitterness, wrath, anger, clamor, and evil speaking be put away from you, with all malice. And be kind to one another, tenderhearted, forgiving one another, even as God in Christ forgave you.

Ephesians 4:31–32

And Naomi said to her two daughters-in-law, "Go, return each to her mother's house. The LORD deal kindly with you, as you have dealt with the dead and with me."

Ruth 1:8

We then who are strong ought to bear with the scruples of the weak, and not to please ourselves.

Romans 15:1

Joseph said to them, "Do not be afraid, for am I in the place of God? But as for you, you meant evil against me; but God meant it for good, in order to bring it about as it is this day, to save many people alive. Now therefore, do not be afraid; I will provide for you and your little ones." And he comforted them and spoke kindly to them.

Genesis 50:19–21

Hatred stirs up strife,
But love covers all sins.

Proverbs 10:12

You are witnesses, and God also, how devoutly and justly and blamelessly we behaved ourselves among you who believe; as you know how we exhorted, and comforted, and charged every one of you, as a father does his own children, that you would walk worthy of God who calls you into His own kingdom and glory.

1 Thessalonians 2:10–12

Trust Him even when you don't understand

Behold, He who keeps Israel
   Shall neither slumber nor sleep.
The LORD is your keeper;
   The LORD is your shade at your right hand.
The sun shall not strike you by day,
   Nor the moon by night.
The LORD shall preserve you from all evil;
   He shall preserve your soul.
The LORD shall preserve your going out and your
     coming in
   From this time forth, and even forevermore.
Psalm 121:4–8

Some trust in chariots, and some in horses;
   But we will remember the name of the LORD
     our God.
They have bowed down and fallen;
   But we have risen and stand upright.
Save, LORD!
   May the King answer us when we call.
Psalm 20:7–9

Even now men cannot look at the light when it
    is bright in the skies,
  When the wind has passed and cleared them.
He comes from the north as golden splendor;
  With God is awesome majesty.
As for the Almighty, we cannot find Him;
  He is excellent in power,
  In judgment and abundant justice;
  He does not oppress.
Therefore men fear Him;
  He shows no partiality to any who are wise
    of heart.

Job 37:21–24

Oh, the depth of the riches both of the wisdom
and knowledge of God! How unsearchable are His
judgments and His ways past finding out!
  "For who has known the mind of the LORD?
  Or who has become His counselor?"
  "Or who has first given to Him
  And it shall be repaid to him?"
For of Him and through Him and to Him are all
things, to whom be glory forever. Amen.

Romans 11:33–36

Then Job answered and said:
"Even today my complaint is bitter;

My hand is listless because of my groaning.
Oh, that I knew where I might find Him,
    That I might come to His seat!
I would present my case before Him,
    And fill my mouth with arguments.
I would know the words which He would
        answer me,
    And understand what He would say to me.
Would He contend with me in His great power?
    No! But He would take note of me.
There the upright could reason with Him,
    And I would be delivered forever from my Judge.
Look, I go forward, but He is not there,
    And backward, but I cannot perceive Him;
When He works on the left hand, I cannot
        behold Him;
    When He turns to the right hand, I cannot
        see Him.
But He knows the way that I take;
    When He has tested me, I shall come forth
        as gold.
My foot has held fast to His steps;
    I have kept His way and not turned aside.
I have not departed from the commandment
        of His lips;
    I have treasured the words of His mouth
    More than my necessary food."

Job 23:1–12

In the day of my trouble I will call upon You,
For You will answer me.
Among the gods there is none like You, O LORD;
Nor are there any works like Your works.
All nations whom You have made
Shall come and worship before You, O LORD,
And shall glorify Your name.
For You are great, and do wondrous things;
You alone are God.

Psalm 86:7–10

Then they cried out to the LORD in their trouble,
And He saved them out of their distresses.
He sent His word and healed them,
And delivered them from their destructions.

Psalm 107:19–20

Every word of God is pure;
He is a shield to those who put their trust
in Him.

Proverbs 30:5

Therefore, brethren, in all our affliction and distress we were comforted concerning you by your faith. For now we live, if you stand fast in the Lord.

1 Thessalonians 3:7–8

Speak encouraging words to all

Therefore, as we have opportunity, let us do good to all, especially to those who are of the household of faith.

Galatians 6:10

Let no corrupt word proceed out of your mouth, but what is good for necessary edification, that it may impart grace to the hearers. And do not grieve the Holy Spirit of God, by whom you were sealed for the day of redemption. Let all bitterness, wrath, anger, clamor, and evil speaking be put away from you, with all malice. And be kind to one another, tenderhearted, forgiving one another, even as God in Christ forgave you.

Ephesians 4:29–32

If anyone among you thinks he is religious, and does not bridle his tongue but deceives his own heart, this one's religion is useless.

James 1:26

Bear one another's burdens, and so fulfill the law of Christ.

Galatians 6:2

For we all stumble in many things. If anyone does not stumble in word, he is a perfect man, able also to bridle the whole body. Indeed, we put bits in horses' mouths that they may obey us, and we turn their whole body. Look also at ships: although they are so large and are driven by fierce winds, they are turned by a very small rudder wherever the pilot desires. Even so the tongue is a little member and boasts great things.

See how great a forest a little fire kindles! And the tongue is a fire, a world of iniquity. The tongue is so set among our members that it defiles the whole body, and sets on fire the course of nature; and it is set on fire by hell. For every kind of beast and bird, of reptile and creature of the sea, is tamed and has been tamed by mankind. But no man can tame the tongue. It is an unruly evil, full of deadly poison. With it we bless our God and Father, and with it we curse men, who have been made in the similitude of God. Out of the same mouth proceed blessing and cursing. My brethren, these things ought not to be so.

James 3:2–10

Not returning evil for evil or reviling for reviling, but on the contrary blessing, knowing that you were called to this, that you may inherit a blessing. For

"He who would love life
And see good days,
Let him refrain his tongue from evil,
And his lips from speaking deceit."

1 Peter 3:9–10

The wilderness and the wasteland shall be glad
  for them,
  And the desert shall rejoice and blossom as
   the rose;
It shall blossom abundantly and rejoice,
  Even with joy and singing.
  The glory of Lebanon shall be given to it,
  The excellence of Carmel and Sharon.
  They shall see the glory of the LORD,
  The excellency of our God.
Strengthen the weak hands,
  And make firm the feeble knees.
Say to those who are fearful-hearted,
  "Be strong, do not fear!
  Behold, your God will come with vengeance,
  With the recompense of God;
  He will come and save you."

Isaiah 35:1–4

A man has joy by the answer of his mouth,
  And a word spoken in due season, how good it is!
                                        Proverbs 15:23

There is one who speaks like the piercings of
    a sword,
  But the tongue of the wise promotes health.
                                        Proverbs 12:18

"For out of the abundance of the heart the mouth speaks. . . .

But I say to you that for every idle word men may speak, they will give account of it in the day of judgment.

For by your words you will be justified, and by your words you will be condemned."
                                        Matthew 12:34, 36–37

We took sweet counsel together,
  And walked to the house of God in the throng.
                                        Psalm 55:14

For none of us lives to himself, and no one dies to himself. For if we live, we live to the Lord; and if we die, we die to the Lord. Therefore, whether we live or die, we are the Lord's. For to this end Christ died and rose and lived again, that He might be Lord of both the dead and the living. But why do you judge your brother? Or why do you show contempt for your brother? For we shall all stand before the judgment seat of Christ. For it is written:

"As I live," says the LORD,

"Every knee shall bow to Me,

And every tongue shall confess to God."

So then each of us shall give account of himself to God. Therefore let us not judge one another anymore, but rather resolve this, not to put a stumbling block or a cause to fall in our brother's way.

I know and am convinced by the Lord Jesus that there is nothing unclean of itself; but to him who considers anything to be unclean, to him it is unclean. Yet if your brother is grieved because of your food, you are no longer walking in love. Do not destroy with your food the one for whom Christ died. Therefore do not let your good be spoken of as evil; for the kingdom of God is not eating and drinking, but righteousness and peace and joy in the Holy Spirit. For he who serves Christ in these things is acceptable to God and approved by men.

Therefore let us pursue the things which make for peace and the things by which one may edify another.

Romans 14:7–19

GOD GIVES YOU
STRENGTH WHEN . . .

You comfort your children in their sorrows

But the mercy of the LORD is from everlasting
    to everlasting
  On those who fear Him,
  And His righteousness to children's children.
Psalm 103:17

He will feed His flock like a shepherd;
  He will gather the lambs with His arm,
  And carry them in His bosom,
  And gently lead those who are with young.
Isaiah 40:11

"Comfort, yes, comfort My people!"
  Says your God. . . .
"The grass withers, the flower fades,
  But the word of our God stands forever."
Isaiah 40:1, 8

Fear not, for I am with you;
   Be not dismayed, for I am your God.
   I will strengthen you,
   Yes, I will help you,
   I will uphold you with My righteous right
      hand. . . .
Behold, I will make you into a new threshing
      sledge with sharp teeth;
   You shall thresh the mountains and beat
      them small,
   And make the hills like chaff.
You shall winnow them, the wind shall carry
      them away,
   And the whirlwind shall scatter them;
   You shall rejoice in the LORD,
   And glory in the Holy One of Israel.
Isaiah 41:10, 15–16

Surely He has borne our griefs
   And carried our sorrows;
   Yet we esteemed Him stricken,
   Smitten by God, and afflicted.
But He was wounded for our transgressions,
   He was bruised for our iniquities;
   The chastisement for our peace was upon Him,
   And by His stripes we are healed.
Isaiah 53:4–5

When the waves of death surrounded me,
  The floods of ungodliness made me afraid.
The sorrows of Sheol surrounded me;
  The snares of death confronted me.
In my distress I called upon the LORD,
  And cried out to my God;
  He heard my voice from His temple,
  And my cry entered His ears.

2 Samuel 22:5–7

Sing, O heavens!
  Be joyful, O earth!
  And break out in singing, O mountains!
  For the LORD has comforted His people,
  And will have mercy on His afflicted.
But Zion said, "The LORD has forsaken me,
  And my Lord has forgotten me."
"Can a woman forget her nursing child,
  And not have compassion on the son of her
    womb?
  Surely they may forget,
  Yet I will not forget you.
See, I have inscribed you on the palms of My
hands;
  Your walls are continually before Me.

Isaiah 49:13–16

The Lord GOD, who gathers the outcasts of
    Israel, says,
  "Yet I will gather to him
  Others besides those who are gathered to him."

Isaiah 56:8

For I have satiated the weary soul, and I have replenished every sorrowful soul.

Jeremiah 31:25

"Are not two sparrows sold for a copper coin? And not one of them falls to the ground apart from your Father's will. But the very hairs of your head are all numbered. Do not fear therefore; you are of more value than many sparrows."

Matthew 10:29–31

Blessed be the God and Father of our Lord Jesus Christ, the Father of mercies and God of all comfort, who comforts us in all our tribulation, that we may be able to comfort those who are in any trouble, with the comfort with which we ourselves are comforted by God. For as the sufferings of Christ abound in us, so our consolation also abounds through Christ.

2 Corinthians 1:3–5

You feel defeated and powerless

God is our refuge and strength,
   A very present help in trouble.
Therefore we will not fear,
   Even though the earth be removed,
   And though the mountains be carried into the
     midst of the sea;
Though its waters roar and be troubled,
   Though the mountains shake with its swelling.
Psalm 46:1–3

Give ear to my words, O LORD,
   Consider my meditation.
Give heed to the voice of my cry,
   My King and my God,
   For to You I will pray.
My voice You shall hear in the morning, O LORD;
   In the morning I will direct it to You,
   And I will look up.
For You are not a God who takes pleasure
    in wickedness,
   Nor shall evil dwell with You.

The boastful shall not stand in Your sight;
  You hate all workers of iniquity.
You shall destroy those who speak falsehood;
    The LORD abhors the bloodthirsty and
      deceitful man.
But as for me, I will come into Your house in the
      multitude of Your mercy;
    In fear of You I will worship toward Your holy
      temple.
Lead me, O LORD, in Your righteousness because
      of my enemies;
    Make Your way straight before my face. . . .
But let all those rejoice who put their trust in You;
    Let them ever shout for joy, because You
      defend them;
    Let those also who love Your name
    Be joyful in You.
For You, O LORD, will bless the righteous;
    With favor You will surround him as with a shield.
                                    Psalm 5:1–8, 11–12

And those who know Your name will put their
      trust in You;
    For You, LORD, have not forsaken those who
      seek You.

                                    Psalm 9:10

Concerning this thing I pleaded with the Lord three times that it might depart from me. And He said to me, "My grace is sufficient for you, for My strength is made perfect in weakness." Therefore most gladly I will rather boast in my infirmities, that the power of Christ may rest upon me. Therefore I take pleasure in infirmities, in reproaches, in needs, in persecutions, in distresses, for Christ's sake. For when I am weak, then I am strong.

2 Corinthians 12:8–10

For affliction does not come from the dust,
    Nor does trouble spring from the ground;
Yet man is born to trouble,
    As the sparks fly upward.
But as for me, I would seek God,
    And to God I would commit my cause—
Who does great things, and unsearchable,
    Marvelous things without number."

Job 5:6–9

You are my hiding place and my shield;
    I hope in Your word.

Psalm 119:114

He who dwells in the secret place of the Most High
    Shall abide under the shadow of the Almighty.
I will say of the LORD, "He is my refuge and
      my fortress;
    My God, in Him I will trust."
Surely He shall deliver you from the snare of
      the fowler
    And from the perilous pestilence.
He shall cover you with His feathers,
    And under His wings you shall take refuge;
    His truth shall be your shield and buckler.
You shall not be afraid of the terror by night,
    Nor of the arrow that flies by day,
Nor of the pestilence that walks in darkness,
    Nor of the destruction that lays waste at noonday.
A thousand may fall at your side,
    And ten thousand at your right hand;
    But it shall not come near you.
Only with your eyes shall you look,
    And see the reward of the wicked.
Because you have made the LORD, who is
      my refuge,
    Even the Most High, your dwelling place,
No evil shall befall you,
    Nor shall any plague come near your dwelling.

Psalm 91:1–10

Give us help from trouble,
For the help of man is useless.
Through God we will do valiantly,
For it is He who shall tread down our enemies.

Psalm 108:12–13

Bow down Your ear, O LORD, hear me;
For I am poor and needy.
Preserve my life, for I am holy;
You are my God;
Save Your servant who trusts in You!
Be merciful to me, O Lord,
For I cry to You all day long.
Rejoice the soul of Your servant,
For to You, O Lord, I lift up my soul.
For You, Lord, are good, and ready to forgive,
And abundant in mercy to all those who call
upon You.
Give ear, O LORD, to my prayer;
And attend to the voice of my supplications.

Psalm 86:1–6

You are my God, and I will praise You;
You are my God, I will exalt You.

Psalm 118:28

I cried out to You, O LORD:
  I said, "You are my refuge,
  My portion in the land of the living.
Attend to my cry,
  For I am brought very low;
  Deliver me from my persecutors,
  For they are stronger than I.
Bring my soul out of prison,
  That I may praise Your name;
  The righteous shall surround me,
  For You shall deal bountifully with me."

Psalm 142:5–7

And I, brethren, when I came to you, did not come with excellence of speech or of wisdom declaring to you the testimony of God. For I determined not to know anything among you except Jesus Christ and Him crucified. I was with you in weakness, in fear, and in much trembling. And my speech and my preaching were not with persuasive words of human wisdom, but in demonstration of the Spirit and of power, that your faith should not be in the wisdom of men but in the power of God.

1 Corinthians 2:1–5

Trouble and anguish have overtaken me,
Yet Your commandments are my delights.
The righteousness of Your testimonies is
everlasting;
Give me understanding, and I shall live.

Psalm 119:143–144

Let this mind be in you which was also in Christ Jesus, who, being in the form of God, did not consider it robbery to be equal with God, But made Himself of no reputation, taking the form of a bondservant, and coming in the likeness of men. And being found in appearance as a man, He humbled Himself and became obedient to the point of death, even the death of the cross. Therefore God also has highly exalted Him and given Him the name which is above every name.

Philippians 2:5–9

Your children disobey you

Children, obey your parents in the Lord, for this is right. . . .

And you, fathers, do not provoke your children to wrath, but bring them up in the training and admonition of the Lord.

Ephesians 6:1, 4

If his sons forsake My law
    And do not walk in My judgments,
If they break My statutes
    And do not keep My commandments,
Then I will punish their transgression with the rod,
    And their iniquity with stripes.
Nevertheless My lovingkindness I will not utterly
        take from him,
    Nor allow My faithfulness to fail.
My covenant I will not break,
    Nor alter the word that has gone out of My lips.

Psalm 89:30–34

But You, O Lord, are a God full of compassion,
    and gracious,
    Longsuffering and abundant in mercy and truth.
Oh, turn to me, and have mercy on me!
    Give Your strength to Your servant,
    And save the son of Your maidservant.

Psalm 86:15–16

Though He was a Son, yet He learned obedience
by the things which He suffered.

Hebrews 5:8

As a father pities his children,
    So the Lord pities those who fear Him.
For He knows our frame;
    He remembers that we are dust.
As for man, his days are like grass;
    As a flower of the field, so he flourishes.
For the wind passes over it, and it is gone,
    And its place remembers it no more.
But the mercy of the Lord is from everlasting
    to everlasting
    On those who fear Him,
    And His righteousness to children's children.

Psalm 103:13–17

We have sinned with our fathers,
   We have committed iniquity,
   We have done wickedly.
Our fathers in Egypt did not understand Your
         wonders;
   They did not remember the multitude of
      Your mercies,
   But rebelled by the sea—the Red Sea.
Nevertheless He saved them for His name's sake,
   That He might make His mighty power known.

Psalm 106:6–8

Many times He delivered them;
   But they rebelled in their counsel,
   And were brought low for their iniquity.
Nevertheless He regarded their affliction,
   When He heard their cry;
And for their sake He remembered His covenant,
   And relented according to the multitude of
      His mercies.

Psalm 106:43–45

Even a child is known by his deeds,
   Whether what he does is pure and right.

Proverbs 20:11

"If you are willing and obedient,
    You shall eat the good of the land;
But if you refuse and rebel,
    You shall be devoured by the sword";
    For the mouth of the LORD has spoken.

Isaiah 1:19–20

Obey those who rule over you, and be submissive, for they watch out for your souls, as those who must give account. Let them do so with joy and not with grief, for that would be unprofitable for you.

Hebrews 13:17

So Samuel said:
    "Has the LORD as great delight in burnt
        offerings and sacrifices,
    As in obeying the voice of the LORD?
    Behold, to obey is better than sacrifice,
    And to heed than the fat of rams.
For rebellion is as the sin of witchcraft,
    And stubbornness is as iniquity and idolatry.
    Because you have rejected the word of the LORD,
    He also has rejected you from being king."

1 Samuel 15:22–23

The proverbs of Solomon:
A wise son makes a glad father,
But a foolish son is the grief of his mother.

Proverbs 10:1

Foolishness is bound up in the heart of a child;
The rod of correction will drive it far from him.

Proverbs 22:15

A wise son heeds his father's instruction,
But a scoffer does not listen to rebuke.

Proverbs 13:1

Likewise you younger people, submit yourselves to your elders. Yes, all of you be submissive to one another, and be clothed with humility, for
"God resists the proud,
But gives grace to the humble."
Therefore humble yourselves under the mighty hand of God, that He may exalt you in due time.

1 Peter 5:5–6

A member of your family dies

He heals the brokenhearted
And binds up their wounds.
He counts the number of the stars;
He calls them all by name.
Great is our Lord, and mighty in power;
His understanding is infinite.

Psalm 147:3–5

But I do not want you to be ignorant, brethren, concerning those who have fallen asleep, lest you sorrow as others who have no hope. For if we believe that Jesus died and rose again, even so God will bring with Him those who sleep in Jesus. For this we say to you by the word of the Lord, that we who are alive and remain until the coming of the Lord will by no means precede those who are asleep. For the Lord Himself will descend from heaven with a shout, with the voice of an archangel, and with the trumpet of God. And the dead in Christ will rise first.

1 Thessalonians 4:13–16

For if the dead do not rise, then Christ is not risen. And if Christ is not risen, your faith is futile; you are still in your sins! Then also those who have fallen asleep in Christ have perished. If in this life only we have hope in Christ, we are of all men the most pitiable.

But now Christ is risen from the dead, and has become the firstfruits of those who have fallen asleep. For since by man came death, by Man also came the resurrection of the dead. For as in Adam all die, even so in Christ all shall be made alive. But each one in his own order: Christ the firstfruits, afterward those who are Christ's at His coming. Then comes the end, when He delivers the kingdom to God the Father, when He puts an end to all rule and all authority and power. For He must reign till He has put all enemies under His feet. The last enemy that will be destroyed is death.

1 Corinthians 15:16–26

Your kingdom is an everlasting kingdom,
    And Your dominion endures throughout all
      generations.
The Lord upholds all who fall,
    And raises up all who are bowed down.

Psalm 145:13–14

To everything there is a season,
    A time for every purpose under heaven:
    A time to be born,
And a time to die;
    A time to plant,
And a time to pluck what is planted;
    A time to kill,
And a time to heal;
    A time to break down,
And a time to build up;
    A time to weep,
And a time to laugh;
    A time to mourn,
And a time to dance;
    A time to cast away stones,
And a time to gather stones;
    A time to embrace,
And a time to refrain from embracing;
    A time to gain,
And a time to lose;
    A time to keep,
And a time to throw away;
    A time to tear,
And a time to sew;
    A time to keep silence,

And a time to speak;
  A time to love,
And a time to hate;
  A time of war,
And a time of peace.

Ecclesiastes 3:1–8

Through the Lord's mercies we are not con-
sumed,
Because His compassions fail not.
  They are new every morning;
Great is Your faithfulness.

Lamentations 33:22–23

Anger threatens
your home's peace

Behold, how good and how pleasant it is
    For brethren to dwell together in unity!
It is like the precious oil upon the head,
    Running down on the beard,
    The beard of Aaron,
    Running down on the edge of his garments.
Psalm 133:1–2

He who is slow to wrath has great understanding,
    But he who is impulsive exalts folly.
Proverbs 14:29

Better is a dinner of herbs where love is,
    Than a fatted calf with hatred.
A wrathful man stirs up strife,
    But he who is slow to anger allays contention.
Proverbs 15:17–18

I am for peace;
  But when I speak, they are for war. . . .
I will lift up my eyes to the hills—
  From whence comes my help?
My help comes from the LORD,
  Who made heaven and earth.
He will not allow your foot to be moved;
  He who keeps you will not slumber.

Psalm 120:7; 121:1–3

He who is slow to anger is better than the mighty,
  And he who rules his spirit than he who takes
    a city.

Proverbs 16:32

The beginning of strife is like releasing water;
  Therefore stop contention before a quarrel starts.

Proverbs 17:14

For God is not the author of confusion but of
peace, as in all the churches of the saints.

1 Corinthians 14:33

So then, my beloved brethren, let every man be swift
to hear, slow to speak, slow to wrath; for the wrath of
man does not produce the righteousness of God.

James 1:19–20

"Be angry, and do not sin": do not let the sun go down on your wrath.

Ephesians 4:26

Hear my prayer, O LORD,
  And let my cry come to You.
Do not hide Your face from me in the day of
    my trouble;
  Incline Your ear to me;
  In the day that I call, answer me speedily.
For my days are consumed like smoke,
  And my bones are burned like a hearth.
My heart is stricken and withered like grass,
  So that I forget to eat my bread.

Psalm 102:1–4

But You, O LORD, shall endure forever,
  And the remembrance of Your name to all
    generations.

Psalm 102:12

Let your speech always be with grace, seasoned with salt, that you may know how you ought to answer each one.

Colossians 4:6

Whoever guards his mouth and tongue
Keeps his soul from troubles.

Proverbs 21:23

Pleasant words are like a honeycomb,
Sweetness to the soul and health to the bones.

Proverbs 16:24

Now I plead with you, brethren, by the name of our Lord Jesus Christ, that you all speak the same thing, and that there be no divisions among you, but that you be perfectly joined together in the same mind and in the same judgment.

1 Corinthians 1:10

Your family grows apart

Children's children are the crown of old men,
And the glory of children is their father.

Proverbs 17:6

Therefore my spirit is overwhelmed within me;
My heart within me is distressed.
I remember the days of old;
I meditate on all Your works;
I muse on the work of Your hands.
I spread out my hands to You;
My soul longs for You like a thirsty land. Selah
Answer me speedily, O Lord;
My spirit fails!
Do not hide Your face from me,
Lest I be like those who go down into the pit.
Cause me to hear Your lovingkindness in the
morning,
For in You do I trust;
Cause me to know the way in which I
should walk,
For I lift up my soul to You.

Psalm 143:4–8

God sets the solitary in families;
　　He brings out those who are bound into
　　　　prosperity;
　　But the rebellious dwell in a dry land.

Psalm 68:6

He who heeds the word wisely will find good,
　　And whoever trusts in the LORD, happy is he.

Proverbs 16:20

A merry heart makes a cheerful countenance,
　　But by sorrow of the heart the spirit is broken.
The heart of him who has understanding seeks
　　　　knowledge,
　　But the mouth of fools feeds on foolishness.
All the days of the afflicted are evil,
　　But he who is of a merry heart has a continual
　　　　feast.
Better is a little with the fear of the LORD,
　　Than great treasure with trouble.

Proverbs 15:13–16

The wise woman builds her house,
　　But the foolish pulls it down with her hands.

Proverbs 14:1

And I, brethren, could not speak to you as to spiritual people but as to carnal, as to babes in Christ. I fed you with milk and not with solid food; for until now you were not able to receive it, and even now you are still not able; for you are still carnal. For where there are envy, strife, and divisions among you, are you not carnal and behaving like mere men?

1 Corinthians 3:1–3

For by one Spirit we were all baptized into one body—whether Jews or Greeks, whether slaves or free—and have all been made to drink into one Spirit. For in fact the body is not one member but many. If the foot should say, "Because I am not a hand, I am not of the body," is it therefore not of the body? And if the ear should say, "Because I am not an eye, I am not of the body," is it therefore not of the body? If the whole body were an eye, where would be the hearing? If the whole were hearing, where would be the smelling? But now God has set the members, each one of them, in the body just as He pleased. And if they were all one member, where would the body be? But now indeed there are many members, yet one body. And the eye cannot say to the hand, "I have no need of you"; nor again the head to the feet, "I have no need of you." No, much rather, those members of the body which seem to be weaker are necessary.

And those members of the body which we think to be less honorable, on these we bestow greater honor; and our unpresentable parts have greater modesty, but our presentable parts have no need. But God composed the body, having given greater honor to that part which lacks it, that there should be no schism in the body, but that the members should have the same care for one another.

And if one member suffers, all the members suffer with it; or if one member is honored, all the members rejoice with it.

1 Corinthians 12:13–26

But Jesus knew their thoughts, and said to them: "Every kingdom divided against itself is brought to desolation, and every city or house divided against itself will not stand."

Matthew 12:25

A brother offended is harder to win than a
    strong city,
  And contentions are like the bars of a castle.

Proverbs 18:19

A merry heart does good, like medicine,
  But a broken spirit dries the bones.

Proverbs 17:22

Better is a dry morsel with quietness,
Than a house full of feasting with strife.

Proverbs 17:1

Pursue peace with all people, and holiness, without which no one will see the Lord: looking carefully lest anyone fall short of the grace of God; lest any root of bitterness springing up cause trouble, and by this many become defiled.

Hebrews 12:14–15

GOD PROTECTS
YOU WHEN . . .

You are concerned about the world's influence on your children

My son, keep your father's command,
  And do not forsake the law of your mother.
Bind them continually upon your heart;
  Tie them around your neck.
When you roam, they will lead you;
  When you sleep, they will keep you;
  And when you awake, they will speak with you.
For the commandment is a lamp,
  And the law a light;
  Reproofs of instruction are the way of life.
Proverbs 6:20–23

Train up a child in the way he should go,
  And when he is old he will not depart from it.
Proverbs 22:6

Whoever keeps the law is a discerning son,
  But a companion of gluttons shames his father.
Proverbs 28:7

"Beware of false prophets, who come to you in sheep's clothing, but inwardly they are ravenous wolves. You will know them by their fruits. Do men gather grapes from thornbushes or figs from thistles? Even so, every good tree bears good fruit, but a bad tree bears bad fruit."

Matthew 7:15–17

For the unbelieving husband is sanctified by the wife, and the unbelieving wife is sanctified by the husband; otherwise your children would be unclean, but now they are holy.

1 Corinthians 7:14

Let no one deceive you with empty words, for because of these things the wrath of God comes upon the sons of disobedience. Therefore do not be partakers with them.

For you were once darkness, but now you are light in the Lord. Walk as children of light (for the fruit of the Spirit is in all goodness, righteousness, and truth), finding out what is acceptable to the Lord. And have no fellowship with the unfruitful works of darkness, but rather expose them. For it is shameful even to speak of those things which are done by them in secret.

Ephesians 5:6 12

Do not be unequally yoked together with unbelievers. For what fellowship has righteousness with lawlessness? And what communion has light with darkness? And what accord has Christ with Belial? Or what part has a believer with an unbeliever? And what agreement has the temple of God with idols? For you are the temple of the living God. As God has said:

"I will dwell in them
And walk among them.
I will be their God,
And they shall be My people."

Therefore

"Come out from among them
And be separate, says the Lord.
Do not touch what is unclean,
And I will receive you."
"I will be a Father to you,
And you shall be My sons and daughters,
Says the Lord Almighty."

2 Corinthians 6:14–18

No temptation has overtaken you except such as is common to man; but God is faithful, who will not allow you to be tempted beyond what you are able, but with the temptation will also make the way of escape, that you may be able to bear it.

1 Corinthians 10:13

Deliver yourself like a gazelle from the hand of
     the hunter,
   And like a bird from the hand of the fowler.
Go to the ant, you sluggard!
   Consider her ways and be wise,
Which, having no captain,
   Overseer or ruler,
Provides her supplies in the summer,
   And gathers her food in the harvest.
How long will you slumber, O sluggard?
   When will you rise from your sleep?
A little sleep, a little slumber,
   A little folding of the hands to sleep—
So shall your poverty come on you like a prowler,
   And your need like an armed man.

Proverbs 6:5–11

When He had called the people to Himself, with
His disciples also, He said to them, "Whoever desires
to come after Me, let him deny himself, and take up
his cross, and follow Me. For whoever desires to save
his life will lose it, but whoever loses his life for My
sake and the gospel's will save it. For what will it profit
a man if he gains the whole world, and loses his own
soul?"

Mark 8:34–36

I beseech you therefore, brethren, by the mercies of God, that you present your bodies a living sacrifice, holy, acceptable to God, which is your reasonable service. And do not be conformed to this world, but be transformed by the renewing of your mind, that you may prove what is that good and acceptable and perfect will of God.

Romans 12:1–2

So shall My word be that goes forth from
 My mouth;
 It shall not return to Me void,
 But it shall accomplish what I please,
 And it shall prosper in the thing for which I
  sent it.
For you shall go out with joy,
 And be led out with peace;
 The mountains and the hills
 Shall break forth into singing before you,
 And all the trees of the field shall clap their hands.
Instead of the thorn shall come up the cypress tree,
 And instead of the brier shall come up the
  myrtle tree;
And it shall be to the LORD for a name,
 For an everlasting sign that shall not be cut off.

Isaiah 55:11–13

You don't know what decisions are best for your family

The steps of a good man are ordered by the LORD,
    And He delights in his way.
Though he fall, he shall not be utterly cast down;
    For the LORD upholds him with His hand.
Psalm 37:23–24

All your children shall be taught by the LORD,
    And great shall be the peace of your children.
Isaiah 54:13

And though the LORD gives you
    The bread of adversity and the water of affliction,
    Yet your teachers will not be moved into a
        corner anymore,
    But your eyes shall see your teachers.
Your ears shall hear a word behind you, saying,
    "This is the way, walk in it,"
    Whenever you turn to the right hand
    Or whenever you turn to the left.
Isaiah 30:20–21

Incline your ear and hear the words of the wise,
    And apply your heart to my knowledge;
For it is a pleasant thing if you keep them
        within you;
    Let them all be fixed upon your lips.

Proverbs 22:17–18

"Now therefore, fear the LORD, serve Him in sincerity and in truth, and put away the gods which your fathers served on the other side of the River and in Egypt. Serve the LORD! "And if it seems evil to you to serve the LORD, choose for yourselves this day whom you will serve, whether the gods which your fathers served that were on the other side of the River, or the gods of the Amorites, in whose land you dwell. But as for me and my house, we will serve the LORD."

So the people answered and said: "Far be it from us that we should forsake the LORD to serve other gods."

Joshua 24:14–16

Do all things without complaining and disputing, that you may become blameless and harmless, children of God without fault in the midst of a crooked and perverse generation, among whom you shine as lights in the world, holding fast the word of life, so that I may rejoice in the day of Christ that I have not run in vain or labored in vain.

Philippians 2:14–16

The LORD will guide you continually,
   And satisfy your soul in drought,
   And strengthen your bones;
   You shall be like a watered garden,
   And like a spring of water, whose waters do
      not fail.
Those from among you
   Shall build the old waste places;
   You shall raise up the foundations of many
      generations;
   And you shall be called the Repairer of the
      Breach,
   The Restorer of Streets to Dwell In.
                              Isaiah 58:11–12

You have dealt well with Your servant,
   O LORD, according to Your word.
Teach me good judgment and knowledge,
   For I believe Your commandments.
                              Psalm 119:65–66

You also gave Your good Spirit to instruct them,
   And did not withhold Your manna from their
      mouth,
   And gave them water for their thirst.
                              Nehemiah 9:20

Trust in the LORD with all your heart,
    And lean not on your own understanding;
In all your ways acknowledge Him,
    And He shall direct your paths.

Proverbs 3:5–6

"Listen to Me, O Jacob,
    And Israel, My called:
    I am He, I am the First,
    I am also the Last.
Indeed My hand has laid the foundation of
        the earth,
    And My right hand has stretched out the
        heavens;
    When I call to them,
    They stand up together. . . .
Come near to Me, hear this:
    I have not spoken in secret from the beginning;
    From the time that it was, I was there.
    And now the Lord GOD and His Spirit
    Have sent Me."
Thus says the LORD, your Redeemer,
    The Holy One of Israel:
    "I am the LORD your God,
    Who teaches you to profit,
    Who leads you by the way you should go."

Isaiah 48:12–13, 16–17

I was so foolish and ignorant;
  I was like a beast before You.
Nevertheless I am continually with You;
  You hold me by my right hand.
You will guide me with Your counsel,
  And afterward receive me to glory.
Whom have I in heaven but You?
  And there is none upon earth that I desire
    besides You.
My flesh and my heart fail;
  But God is the strength of my heart and my
    portion forever.

Psalm 73:22–26

You question God's power to meet all situations

~~~❦~~~

For our gospel did not come to you in word only, but also in power, and in the Holy Spirit and in much assurance, as you know what kind of men we were among you for your sake.

1 Thessalonians 1:5

Now may the God of peace Himself sanctify you completely; and may your whole spirit, soul, and body be preserved blameless at the coming of our Lord Jesus Christ. He who calls you is faithful, who also will do it.

1 Thessalonians 5:23–24

Behold, happy is the man whom God corrects;
  Therefore do not despise the chastening of
    the Almighty.
For He bruises, but He binds up;
  He wounds, but His hands make whole.
He shall deliver you in six troubles,
  Yes, in seven no evil shall touch you.

In famine He shall redeem you from death,
    And in war from the power of the sword.
You shall be hidden from the scourge of the tongue,
    And you shall not be afraid of destruction
        when it comes.
You shall laugh at destruction and famine,
    And you shall not be afraid of the beasts of
        the earth.
For you shall have a covenant with the stones of
        the field,
    And the beasts of the field shall be at peace
        with you.
You shall know that your tent is in peace;
    You shall visit your dwelling and find nothing
        amiss.
You shall also know that your descendants shall
        be many,
    And your offspring like the grass of the earth.
You shall come to the grave at a full age,
    As a sheaf of grain ripens in its season.
Behold, this we have searched out;
    It is true.
    Hear it, and know for yourself.

Job 5:17–27

For this reason we also, since the day we heard it, do not cease to pray for you, and to ask that you may be filled with the knowledge of His will in all wisdom and spiritual understanding; that you may walk worthy of the Lord, fully pleasing Him, being fruitful in every good work and increasing in the knowledge of God; strengthened with all might, according to His glorious power, for all patience and longsuffering with joy; giving thanks to the Father who has qualified us to be partakers of the inheritance of the saints in the light. He has delivered us from the power of darkness and conveyed us into the kingdom of the Son of His love.

Colossians 1:9–13

Now when He got into a boat, His disciples followed Him. And suddenly a great tempest arose on the sea, so that the boat was covered with the waves. But He was asleep. Then His disciples came to Him and awoke Him, saying, "Lord, save us! We are perishing!"

But He said to them, "Why are you fearful, O you of little faith?" Then He arose and rebuked the winds and the sea, and there was a great calm. So the men marveled, saying, "Who can this be, that even the winds and the sea obey Him?"

Matthew 8:23–27

And the apostles said to the Lord, "Increase our faith."

So the Lord said, "If you have faith as a mustard seed, you can say to this mulberry tree, 'Be pulled up by the roots and be planted in the sea,' and it would obey you."

Luke 17:5–6

Therefore I also, after I heard of your faith in the Lord Jesus and your love for all the saints, do not cease to give thanks for you, making mention of you in my prayers: that the God of our Lord Jesus Christ, the Father of glory, may give to you the spirit of wisdom and revelation in the knowledge of Him, the eyes of your understanding being enlightened; that you may know what is the hope of His calling, what are the riches of the glory of His inheritance in the saints, and what is the exceeding greatness of His power toward us who believe, according to the working of His mighty power which He worked in Christ when He raised Him from the dead and seated Him at His right hand in the heavenly places, far above all principality and power and might and dominion, and every name that is named, not only in this age but also in that which is to come.

And He put all things under His feet, and gave Him to be head over all things to the church, which is His body, the fullness of Him who fills all in all.

Ephesians 1:15–23

You feel depressed and lose your way

Now faith is the substance of things hoped for, the evidence of things not seen. For by it the elders obtained a good testimony.

By faith we understand that the worlds were framed by the word of God, so that the things which are seen were not made of things which are visible. . . .

These all died in faith, not having received the promises, but having seen them afar off were assured of them, embraced them and confessed that they were strangers and pilgrims on the earth.

Hebrews 11:1–3, 13

You have not yet resisted to bloodshed, striving against sin. And you have forgotten the exhortation which speaks to you as to sons:

"My son, do not despise the chastening of the LORD,
Nor be discouraged when you are rebuked by Him;
For whom the LORD loves He chastens,
And scourges every son whom He receives."

Hebrews 12:4–6

Then the Lord knows how to deliver the godly out of temptations and to reserve the unjust under punishment for the day of judgment.

2 Peter 2:9

For you have need of endurance, so that after you have done the will of God, you may receive the promise:
"For yet a little while,
And He who is coming will come and will not tarry."

Hebrews 10:36–37

"Whoever seeks to save his life will lose it, and whoever loses his life will preserve it."

Luke 17:33

Nevertheless He saved them for His name's sake,
That He might make His mighty power known.

Psalm 106:8

So we may boldly say:
"The LORD is my helper;
I will not fear.
What can man do to me?"

Hebrews 13:6

Therefore submit to God. Resist the devil and he will flee from you. Draw near to God and He will draw near to you. Cleanse your hands, you sinners; and purify your hearts, you double-minded. Lament and mourn and weep! Let your laughter be turned to mourning and your joy to gloom. Humble yourselves in the sight of the Lord, and He will lift you up.

James 4:7–10

Blessed is the man who endures temptation; for when he has been approved, he will receive the crown of life which the Lord has promised to those who love Him. Let no one say when he is tempted, "I am tempted by God"; for God cannot be tempted by evil, nor does He Himself tempt anyone. But each one is tempted when he is drawn away by his own desires and enticed. Then, when desire has conceived, it gives birth to sin; and sin, when it is full-grown, brings forth death.

Do not be deceived, my beloved brethren.

James 1:12–16

Yet if anyone suffers as a Christian, let him not be ashamed, but let him glorify God in this matter. . . .

Therefore let those who suffer according to the will of God commit their souls to Him in doing good, as to a faithful Creator.

1 Peter 4:16, 19

Having a good conscience, that when they defame you as evildoers, those who revile your good conduct in Christ may be ashamed. For it is better, if it is the will of God, to suffer for doing good than for doing evil.

For Christ also suffered once for sins, the just for the unjust, that He might bring us to God, being put to death in the flesh but made alive by the Spirit.

1 Peter 3:16–18

My little children, these things I write to you, so that you may not sin. And if anyone sins, we have an Advocate with the Father, Jesus Christ the righteous. And He Himself is the propitiation for our sins, and not for ours only but also for the whole world.

1 John 2:1–2

GOD CHALLENGES
YOU TO . . .

Teach your children to love God

Jesus answered and said to him, "Most assuredly, I say to you, unless one is born again, he cannot see the kingdom of God."

Nicodemus said to Him, "How can a man be born when he is old? Can he enter a second time into his mother's womb and be born?"

Jesus answered, "Most assuredly, I say to you, unless one is born of water and the Spirit, he cannot enter the kingdom of God. That which is born of the flesh is flesh, and that which is born of the Spirit is spirit. Do not marvel that I said to you, 'You must be born again.'"

John 3:3–7

Then little children were brought to Him that He might put His hands on them and pray, but the disciples rebuked them. But Jesus said, "Let the little children come to Me, and do not forbid them; for of such is the kingdom of heaven." And He laid His hands on them and departed from there.

Matthew 19:13–15

I write to you, little children,
Because your sins are forgiven you for His
name's sake.
I write to you, fathers,
Because you have known Him who is from
the beginning.
I write to you, young men,
Because you have overcome the wicked one.
I write to you, little children,
Because you have known the Father.
I have written to you, fathers,
Because you have known Him who is from
the beginning.
I have written to you, young men,
Because you are strong, and the word of God
abides in you,
And you have overcome the wicked one.

Do not love the world or the things in the world. If anyone loves the world, the love of the Father is not in him. For all that is in the world—the lust of the flesh, the lust of the eyes, and the pride of life—is not of the Father but is of the world. And the world is passing away, and the lust of it; but he who does the will of God abides forever.

1 John 2:12–17

Beloved, let us love one another, for love is of God; and everyone who loves is born of God and knows God. He who does not love does not know God, for God is love. In this the love of God was manifested toward us, that God has sent His only begotten Son into the world, that we might live through Him. In this is love, not that we loved God, but that He loved us and sent His Son to be the propitiation for our sins. Beloved, if God so loved us, we also ought to love one another.

No one has seen God at any time. If we love one another, God abides in us, and His love has been perfected in us. By this we know that we abide in Him, and He in us, because He has given us of His Spirit. And we have seen and testify that the Father has sent the Son as Savior of the world. Whoever confesses that Jesus is the Son of God, God abides in him, and he in God. And we have known and believed the love that God has for us. God is love, and he who abides in love abides in God, and God in him.

Love has been perfected among us in this: that we may have boldness in the day of judgment; because as He is, so are we in this world. There is no fear in love; but perfect love casts out fear, because fear involves torment. But he who fears has not been made perfect in love. We love Him because He first loved us.

If someone says, "I love God," and hates his brother, he is a liar; for he who does not love his brother whom he has seen, how can he love God whom he has not seen? And this commandment we have from Him: that he who loves God must love his brother also.

1 John 4:7–21

He came to His own, and His own did not receive Him. But as many as received Him, to them He gave the right to become children of God, to those who believe in His name.

John 1:11–12

Grow in your own
Christian walk

The Elder,

To the beloved Gaius, whom I love in truth: Beloved, I pray that you may prosper in all things and be in health, just as your soul prospers. For I rejoiced greatly when brethren came and testified of the truth that is in you, just as you walk in the truth. I have no greater joy than to hear that my children walk in truth.

3 John 1–4

Now by this we know that we know Him, if we keep His commandments. He who says, "I know Him," and does not keep His commandments, is a liar, and the truth is not in him. But whoever keeps His word, truly the love of God is perfected in him. By this we know that we are in Him. He who says he abides in Him ought himself also to walk just as He walked.

1 John 2:3–6

Teach me, O LORD, the way of Your statutes,
    And I shall keep it to the end.
Give me understanding, and I shall keep Your law;
    Indeed, I shall observe it with my whole heart.
Make me walk in the path of Your commandments,
    For I delight in it.

Psalm 119:33–35

Your word is a lamp to my feet
    And a light to my path.
I have sworn and confirmed
    That I will keep Your righteous judgments.
I am afflicted very much;
    Revive me, O LORD, according to Your word.
Accept, I pray, the freewill offerings of my mouth,
    O LORD,
    And teach me Your judgments.
My life is continually in my hand,
    Yet I do not forget Your law.

Psalm 119:105–109

Therefore, having these promises, beloved, let us cleanse ourselves from all filthiness of the flesh and spirit, perfecting holiness in the fear of God.

2 Corinthians 7:1

Teach me Your way, O Lord;
   I will walk in Your truth;
   Unite my heart to fear Your name.
I will praise You, O Lord my God, with all my
      heart,
   And I will glorify Your name forevermore.

Psalm 86:11–12

You cannot drink the cup of the Lord and the cup of demons; you cannot partake of the Lord's table and of the table of demons. Or do we provoke the Lord to jealousy? Are we stronger than He?

All things are lawful for me, but not all things are helpful; all things are lawful for me, but not all things edify.

1 Corinthians 10:21–23

That the righteous requirement of the law might be fulfilled in us who do not walk according to the flesh but according to the Spirit. For those who live according to the flesh set their minds on the things of the flesh, but those who live according to the Spirit, the things of the Spirit. For to be carnally minded is death, but to be spiritually minded is life and peace.

Romans 8:4–6

Because it is written, "Be holy, for I am holy."

1 Peter 1:16

"Two men went up to the temple to pray, one a Pharisee and the other a tax collector. The Pharisee stood and prayed thus with himself, 'God, I thank You that I am not like other men—extortioners, unjust, adulterers, or even as this tax collector. I fast twice a week; I give tithes of all that I possess.' And the tax collector, standing afar off, would not so much as raise his eyes to heaven, but beat his breast, saying, 'God, be merciful to me a sinner!' I tell you, this man went down to his house justified rather than the other; for everyone who exalts himself will be humbled, and he who humbles himself will be exalted."

Luke 18:10–14

And do this, knowing the time, that now it is high time to awake out of sleep; for now our salvation is nearer than when we first believed. The night is far spent, the day is at hand. Therefore let us cast off the works of darkness, and let us put on the armor of light. Let us walk properly, as in the day, not in revelry and drunkenness, not in lewdness and lust, not in strife and envy. But put on the Lord Jesus Christ, and make no provision for the flesh, to fulfill its lusts.

Romans 13:11–14

Apply your heart to instruction,
And your ears to words of knowledge.

Proverbs 23:12

Fight the good fight of faith, lay hold on eternal life, to which you were also called and have confessed the good confession in the presence of many witnesses.

1 Timothy 6:12

Whoever believes that Jesus is the Christ is born of God, and everyone who loves Him who begot also loves him who is begotten of Him. By this we know that we love the children of God, when we love God and keep His commandments. For this is the love of God, that we keep His commandments. And His commandments are not burdensome.

1 John 5:1–3

Share your faith
with your children

━━━◦❦◦━━━

And these words which I command you today shall
be in your heart. You shall teach them diligently to
your children, and shall talk of them when you sit
in your house, when you walk by the way, when you
lie down, and when you rise up. You shall bind them
as a sign on your hand, and they shall be as frontlets
between your eyes. You shall write them on the door-
posts of your house and on your gates.

Deuteronomy 6:6–9

But before faith came, we were kept under guard
by the law, kept for the faith which would afterward
be revealed. Therefore the law was our tutor to bring
us to Christ, that we might be justified by faith. But
after faith has come, we are no longer under a tutor.

For you are all sons of God through faith in Christ
Jesus. For as many of you as were baptized into Christ
have put on Christ.

Galatians 3:23–27

Then Jesus called a little child to Him, set him in the midst of them, and said, "Assuredly, I say to you, unless you are converted and become as little children, you will by no means enter the kingdom of heaven. Therefore whoever humbles himself as this little child is the greatest in the kingdom of heaven. Whoever receives one little child like this in My name receives Me.

"Whoever causes one of these little ones who believe in Me to sin, it would be better for him if a millstone were hung around his neck, and he were drowned in the depth of the sea. . . .

"Take heed that you do not despise one of these little ones, for I say to you that in heaven their angels always see the face of My Father who is in heaven.

For the Son of Man has come to save that which was lost.

"What do you think? If a man has a hundred sheep, and one of them goes astray, does he not leave the ninety-nine and go to the mountains to seek the one that is straying? And if he should find it, assuredly, I say to you, he rejoices more over that sheep than over the ninety-nine that did not go astray. Even so it is not the will of your Father who is in heaven that one of these little ones should perish."

Matthew 18:2–6, 10–14

But what does it say? "The word is near you, in your mouth and in your heart" (that is, the word of faith which we preach): that if you confess with your mouth the Lord Jesus and believe in your heart that God has raised Him from the dead, you will be saved. For with the heart one believes unto righteousness, and with the mouth confession is made unto salvation. For the Scripture says, "Whoever believes on Him will not be put to shame."

Romans 10:8–11

For this is good and acceptable in the sight of God our Savior, who desires all men to be saved and to come to the knowledge of the truth.

1 Timothy 2:3–4

For the equipping of the saints for the work of ministry, for the edifying of the body of Christ, till we all come to the unity of the faith and of the knowledge of the Son of God, to a perfect man, to the measure of the stature of the fullness of Christ; that we should no longer be children, tossed to and fro and carried about with every wind of doctrine, by the trickery of men, in the cunning craftiness of deceitful plotting, but, speaking the truth in love, may grow up in all things into Him who is the head—Christ.

Ephesians 4:12–15

And the keeper of the prison, awaking from sleep and seeing the prison doors open, supposing the prisoners had fled, drew his sword and was about to kill himself. But Paul called with a loud voice, saying, "Do yourself no harm, for we are all here."

Then he called for a light, ran in, and fell down trembling before Paul and Silas. And he brought them out and said, "Sirs, what must I do to be saved?"

So they said, "Believe on the Lord Jesus Christ, and you will be saved, you and your household." Then they spoke the word of the Lord to him and to all who were in his house. And he took them the same hour of the night and washed their stripes. And immediately he and all his family were baptized.

Acts 16:27–33

Then they brought little children to Him, that He might touch them; but the disciples rebuked those who brought them. But when Jesus saw it, He was greatly displeased and said to them, "Let the little children come to Me, and do not forbid them; for of such is the kingdom of God. "Assuredly, I say to you, whoever does not receive the kingdom of God as a little child will by no means enter it." And He took them up in His arms, laid His hands on them, and blessed them.

Mark 10:13–16

Brethren, if anyone among you wanders from the truth, and someone turns him back, let him know that he who turns a sinner from the error of his way will save a soul from death and cover a multitude of sins.

James 5:19–20

Deal honestly with those close to you

The fathers have eaten sour grapes,
And the children's teeth are set on edge.

Jeremiah 31:29

"Judge not, that you be not judged. For with what judgment you judge, you will be judged; and with the measure you use, it will be measured back to you. And why do you look at the speck in your brother's eye, but do not consider the plank in your own eye? Or how can you say to your brother, 'Let me remove the speck from your eye'; and look, a plank is in your own eye? Hypocrite! First remove the plank from your own eye, and then you will see clearly to remove the speck from your brother's eye."

Matthew 7:1–5

Do not lie to one another, since you have put off the old man with his deeds, and have put on the new man who is renewed in knowledge according to the image of Him who created him.

Colossians 3:9–10

Then the LORD sent Nathan to David. And he came to him, and said to him: "There were two men in one city, one rich and the other poor. The rich man had exceedingly many flocks and herds. But the poor man had nothing, except one little ewe lamb which he had bought and nourished; and it grew up together with him and with his children. It ate of his own food and drank from his own cup and lay in his bosom; and it was like a daughter to him. And a traveler came to the rich man, who refused to take from his own flock and from his own herd to prepare one for the wayfaring man who had come to him; but he took the poor man's lamb and prepared it for the man who had come to him."

So David's anger was greatly aroused against the man, and he said to Nathan, "As the Lord lives, the man who has done this shall surely die! And he shall restore fourfold for the lamb, because he did this thing and because he had no pity."

Then Nathan said to David, "You are the man!"

2 Samuel 12:1–7

Do not withhold good from those to whom it is due,
When it is in the power of your hand to do so.

Proverbs 3:27

He who is often rebuked, and hardens his neck,
  Will suddenly be destroyed, and that without
    remedy.

Proverbs 29:1

Lying lips are an abomination to the LORD,
  But those who deal truthfully are His delight.
Proverbs 12:22

If indeed you have heard Him and have been taught by Him, as the truth is in Jesus: that you put off, concerning your former conduct, the old man which grows corrupt according to the deceitful lusts, and be renewed in the spirit of your mind, and that you put on the new man which was created according to God, in true righteousness and holiness.

Therefore, putting away lying, "Let each one of you speak truth with his neighbor," for we are members of one another.

Ephesians 4:21–25

And take not the word of truth utterly out of
    my mouth,
  For I have hoped in Your ordinances.
So shall I keep Your law continually,
  Forever and ever.
And I will walk at liberty,
  For I seek Your precepts.

Psalm 119:43–45

Ask forgiveness when you wrong your family

And he will turn
> The hearts of the fathers to the children,
> And the hearts of the children to their fathers,
> Lest I come and strike the earth with a curse.

Malachi 4:6

He who covers his sins will not prosper,
> But whoever confesses and forsakes them will
> have mercy.

Proverbs 28:13

"Take heed to yourselves. If your brother sins against you, rebuke him; and if he repents, forgive him. And if he sins against you seven times in a day, and seven times in a day returns to you, saying, 'I repent,' you shall forgive him."

Luke 17:3–4

A man's pride will bring him low,
But the humble in spirit will retain honor.

Proverbs 29:23

"And whenever you stand praying, if you have anything against anyone, forgive him, that your Father in heaven may also forgive you your trespasses. But if you do not forgive, neither will your Father in heaven forgive your trespasses."

Mark 11:25–26

The righteous man walks in his integrity;
His children are blessed after him.

Proverbs 20:7

I, therefore, the prisoner of the Lord, beseech you to walk worthy of the calling with which you were called, with all lowliness and gentleness, with longsuffering, bearing with one another in love, endeavoring to keep the unity of the Spirit in the bond of peace.

Ephesians 4:1–3

Bearing with one another, and forgiving one another, if anyone has a complaint against another; even as Christ forgave you, so you also must do.

Colossians 3:13

"For if you forgive men their trespasses, your heavenly Father will also forgive you. But if you do not forgive men their trespasses, neither will your Father forgive your trespasses."

Matthew 6:14–15

And [the son] arose and came to his father. But when he was still a great way off, his father saw him and had compassion, and ran and fell on his neck and kissed him. And the son said to him, "Father, I have sinned against heaven and in your sight, and am no longer worthy to be called your son."

But the father said to his servants, "Bring out the best robe and put it on him, and put a ring on his hand and sandals on his feet. And bring the fatted calf here and kill it, and let us eat and be merry; for this my son was dead and is alive again; he was lost and is found."

Luke 15:20–24

Never stop loving your wife

Live joyfully with the wife whom you love all the days of your vain life which He has given you under the sun, all your days of vanity; for that is your portion in life, and in the labor which you perform under the sun.

Ecclesiastes 9:9

Many waters cannot quench love,
    Nor can the floods drown it.
    If a man would give for love
    All the wealth of his house,
    It would be utterly despised.

Song of Solomon 8:7

He who finds a wife finds a good thing,
    And obtains favor from the LORD.

Proverbs 18:22

Who satisfies your mouth with good things,
    So that your youth is renewed like the eagle's.

Psalm 103:5

Let your fountain be blessed,
    And rejoice with the wife of your youth.
As a loving deer and a graceful doe,
    Let her breasts satisfy you at all times;
    And always be enraptured with her love.

Proverbs 5:18–19

And He answered and said to them, "Have you not read that He who made them at the beginning 'made them male and female,' and said, 'For this reason a man shall leave his father and mother and be joined to his wife, and the two shall become one flesh'? So then, they are no longer two but one flesh. Therefore what God has joined together, let not man separate."

Matthew 19:4–6

And the LORD God said, "It is not good that man should be alone; I will make him a helper comparable to him."

Genesis 2:18

How fair is your love,
    My sister, my spouse!
    How much better than wine is your love,
    And the scent of your perfumes
    Than all spices!

Your lips, O my spouse,
　　Drip as the honeycomb;
　　Honey and milk are under your tongue;
　　And the fragrance of your garments
　　Is like the fragrance of Lebanon.
A garden enclosed
　　Is my sister, my spouse,
　　A spring shut up,
　　A fountain sealed.
Your plants are an orchard of pomegranates
　　With pleasant fruits,
　　Fragrant henna with spikenard,
Spikenard and saffron,
　　Calamus and cinnamon,
　　With all trees of frankincense,
　　Myrrh and aloes,
　　With all the chief spices—
A fountain of gardens,
　　A well of living waters,
　　And streams from Lebanon.
Awake, O north wind,
　　And come, O south!
　　Blow upon my garden,
　　That its spices may flow out.
　　Let my beloved come to his garden
　　And eat its pleasant fruits.

Song of Solomon 4:10–16

"But from the beginning of the creation, God 'made them male and female. For this reason a man shall leave his father and mother and be joined to his wife, and the two shall become one flesh'; so then they are no longer two, but one flesh. Therefore what God has joined together, let not man separate."

Mark 10:6–9

Nevertheless, because of sexual immorality, let each man have his own wife, and let each woman have her own husband. Let the husband render to his wife the affection due her, and likewise also the wife to her husband. The wife does not have authority over her own body, but the husband does. And likewise the husband does not have authority over his own body, but the wife does. Do not deprive one another except with consent for a time, that you may give yourselves to fasting and prayer; and come together again so that Satan does not tempt you because of your lack of self-control. But I say this as a concession, not as a commandment.

1 Corinthians 7:2–6

Marriage is honorable among all, and the bed undefiled; but fornicators and adulterers God will judge.

Hebrews 13:4

And the LORD God caused a deep sleep to fall on Adam, and he slept; and He took one of his ribs, and closed up the flesh in its place. Then the rib which the LORD God had taken from man He made into a woman, and He brought her to the man.

And Adam said:

"This is now bone of my bones
And flesh of my flesh;
She shall be called Woman,
Because she was taken out of Man."

Therefore a man shall leave his father and mother and be joined to his wife, and they shall become one flesh.

And they were both naked, the man and his wife, and were not ashamed.

Genesis 2:21–25

Houses and riches are an inheritance from fathers,
But a prudent wife is from the LORD.

Proverbs 19:14

Be wise with your family's finances

Now it shall come to pass, if you diligently obey the voice of the LORD your God, to observe carefully all His commandments which I command you today, that the LORD your God will set you high above all nations of the earth. And all these blessings shall come upon you and overtake you, because you obey the voice of the LORD your God:

Blessed shall you be in the city, and blessed shall you be in the country.

Blessed shall be the fruit of your body, the produce of your ground and the increase of your herds, the increase of your cattle and the offspring of your flocks.

Blessed shall be your basket and your kneading bowl.

Blessed shall you be when you come in, and blessed shall you be when you go out.

Deuteronomy 28:1–6

Behold, My Servant shall deal prudently;
He shall be exalted and extolled and be very high.

Isaiah 52:13

But if anyone does not provide for his own, and especially for those of his household, he has denied the faith and is worse than an unbeliever.

1 Timothy 5:8

And you shall remember the LORD your God, for it is He who gives you power to get wealth, that He may establish His covenant which He swore to your fathers, as it is this day.

Deuteronomy 8:18

If they obey and serve Him,
    They shall spend their days in prosperity,
    And their years in pleasures.

Job 36:11

Trust in the LORD, and do good;
    Dwell in the land, and feed on His faithfulness.
    Delight yourself also in the LORD,
    And He shall give you the desires of your heart.
Commit your way to the LORD,
    Trust also in Him,
    And He shall bring it to pass.

Psalm 37:3–5

For "the earth is the LORD's, and all its fullness."

1 Corinthians 10:26

I went by the field of the lazy man,
    And by the vineyard of the man devoid of
        understanding;
And there it was, all overgrown with thorns;
    Its surface was covered with nettles;
    Its stone wall was broken down.
When I saw it, I considered it well;
    I looked on it and received instruction:
A little sleep, a little slumber,
    A little folding of the hands to rest;
So shall your poverty come like a prowler,
    And your need like an armed man.

Proverbs 24:30–34

The lazy man will not plow because of winter;
    He will beg during harvest and have nothing.

Proverbs 20:4

Then you will prosper, if you take care to fulfill the statutes and judgments with which the LORD charged Moses concerning Israel. Be strong and of good courage; do not fear nor be dismayed.

1 Chronicles 22:13

"So that you do not appear to men to be fasting, but to your Father who is in the secret place; and your Father who sees in secret will reward you openly.

"Do not lay up for yourselves treasures on earth, where moth and rust destroy and where thieves break in and steal; but lay up for yourselves treasures in heaven, where neither moth nor rust destroys and where thieves do not break in and steal. For where your treasure is, there your heart will be also."

Matthew 6:18–21

The LORD makes poor and makes rich;
    He brings low and lifts up.
He raises the poor from the dust
    And lifts the beggar from the ash heap,
    To set them among princes
    And make them inherit the throne of glory.
    For the pillars of the earth are the LORD's,
    And He has set the world upon them.
He will guard the feet of His saints,
    But the wicked shall be silent in darkness.
    For by strength no man shall prevail.

1 Samuel 2:7–9

Better is a little with righteousness,
    Than vast revenues without justice.

Proverbs 16:8

For the love of money is a root of all kinds of evil, for which some have strayed from the faith in their greediness, and pierced themselves through with many sorrows.

1 Timothy 6:10

Do not be one of those who sakes hands in
    a pledge,
One of those who is surety for debts;
If you have nothing with which to pay. . . .

Proverbs 22:26–27

Bring your tithe into the storehouse

The righteous shall flourish like a palm tree,
He shall grow like a cedar in Lebanon.

Psalm 92:12

"Give, and it will be given to you: good measure,
pressed down, shaken together, and running over will
be put into your bosom. For with the same measure
that you use, it will be measured back to you."

Luke 6:38

Three times a year all your males shall appear
before the LORD your God in the place which He
chooses: at the Feast of Unleavened Bread, at the Feast
of Weeks, and at the Feast of Tabernacles; and they
shall not appear before the LORD empty-handed.

Every man shall give as he is able, according to the
blessing of the LORD your God which He has given
you.

Deuteronomy 16:16–17

"Will a man rob God?
    Yet you have robbed Me!
    But you say,
    'In what way have we robbed You?'
    In tithes and offerings.
You are cursed with a curse,
    For you have robbed Me,
    Even this whole nation.
Bring all the tithes into the storehouse,
    That there may be food in My house,
    And try Me now in this,"
    Says the LORD of hosts,
    "If I will not open for you the windows of
        heaven
    And pour out for you such blessing
    That there will not be room enough to receive it.
And I will rebuke the devourer for your sakes,
    So that he will not destroy the fruit of your
        ground,
    Nor shall the vine fail to bear fruit for you in
        the field,"
    Says the LORD of hosts;
"And all nations will call you blessed,
    For you will be a delightful land,"
    Says the LORD of hosts.

Malachi 3:8–12

Honor the LORD with your possessions,
    And with the firstfruits of all your increase;
So your barns will be filled with plenty,
    And your vats will overflow with new wine.

Proverbs 3:9–10

But this I say: He who sows sparingly will also reap sparingly, and he who sows bountifully will also reap bountifully. So let each one give as he purposes in his heart, not grudgingly or of necessity; for God loves a cheerful giver. And God is able to make all grace abound toward you, that you, always having all sufficiency in all things, may have an abundance for every good work. As it is written:

"He has dispersed abroad,
He has given to the poor;
His righteousness endures forever."

Now may He who supplies seed to the sower, and bread for food, supply and multiply the seed you have sown and increase the fruits of your righteousness, while you are enriched in everything for all liberality, which causes thanksgiving through us to God. For the administration of this service not only supplies the needs of the saints, but also is abounding through many thanksgivings to God.

2 Corinthians 9:6–12

Now concerning the collection for the saints, as I have given orders to the churches of Galatia, so you must do also: On the first day of the week let each one of you lay something aside, storing up as he may prosper, that there be no collections when I come.

1 Corinthians 16:1–2

Give to the LORD, O families of the peoples,
  Give to the LORD glory and strength.
Give to the LORD the glory due His name;
  Bring an offering, and come into His courts.
Oh, worship the LORD in the beauty of holiness!
  Tremble before Him, all the earth.

Psalm 96:7–9

GOD LISTENS
TO YOUR
PRAYERS WHEN . . .

Your children disappoint you

A wise servant will rule over a son who
    causes shame,
      And will share an inheritance among the brothers.

Proverbs 17:2

For if the firstfruit is holy, the lump is also holy;
and if the root is holy, so are the branches.

Romans 11:16

(For the LORD your God is a merciful God), He
will not forsake you nor destroy you, nor forget the
covenant of your fathers which He swore to them.

Deuteronomy 4:31

Those who are planted in the house of the LORD
    Shall flourish in the courts of our God.
They shall still bear fruit in old age;
    They shall be fresh and flourishing,
To declare that the LORD is upright;
    He is my rock, and there is no unrighteousness
      in Him.

Psalm 92:13–15

Then I said, "I have labored in vain,
> I have spent my strength for nothing and in vain;
> Yet surely my just reward is with the LORD,
> And my work with my God." . . .

Thus says the LORD:
> "In an acceptable time I have heard You,
> And in the day of salvation I have helped You;
> I will preserve You and give You
> As a covenant to the people,
> To restore the earth,
> To cause them to inherit the desolate heritages;

That You may say to the prisoners, 'Go forth,'
> To those who are in darkness, 'Show yourselves.'
> They shall feed along the roads,
> And their pastures shall be on all desolate
>> heights.

They shall neither hunger nor thirst,
> Neither heat nor sun shall strike them;
> For He who has mercy on them will lead them,
> Even by the springs of water He will guide them.

I will make each of My mountains a road, and My
> highways shall be elevated."

Isaiah 49:4, 8–11

Who would form a god or mold an image
> That profits him nothing?

Isaiah 44:10

Now the sons of Eli were corrupt; they did not know the LORD. And the priests' custom with the people was that when any man offered a sacrifice, the priest's servant would come with a three-pronged fleshhook in his hand while the meat was boiling. . . .

Also, before they burned the fat, the priest's servant would come and say to the man who sacrificed, "Give meat for roasting to the priest, for he will not take boiled meat from you, but raw."

And if the man said to him, "They should really burn the fat first; then you may take as much as your heart desires," he would then answer him, "No, but you must give it now; and if not, I will take it by force."

Therefore the sin of the young men was very great before the LORD, for men abhorred the offering of the LORD. . . .

Now Eli was very old; and he heard everything his sons did to all Israel, and how they lay with the women who assembled at the door of the tabernacle of meeting. So he said to them, "Why do you do such things? For I hear of your evil dealings from all the people. No, my sons! For it is not a good report that I hear. You make the LORD's people transgress. If one man sins against another, God will judge him. But if a man sins against the LORD, who will intercede for him?" Nevertheless they did not heed the voice of their father, because the LORD desired to kill them.

1 Samuel 2:12–13, 15–17, 22–25

For I know of nothing against myself, yet I am not justified by this; but He who judges me is the Lord. Therefore judge nothing before the time, until the Lord comes, who will both bring to light the hidden things of darkness and reveal the counsels of the hearts. Then each one's praise will come from God.

1 Corinthians 4:4–5

He heals the brokenhearted
  And binds up their wounds.

Psalm 147:3

Just then the Cushite came, and the Cushite said, "There is good news, my lord the king! For the LORD has avenged you this day of all those who rose against you."

And the king said to the Cushite, "Is the young man Absalom safe?"

So the Cushite answered, "May the enemies of my lord the king, and all who rise against you to do harm, be like that young man!"

Then the king was deeply moved, and went up to the chamber over the gate, and wept. And as he went, he said thus: "O my son Absalom—my son, my son Absalom—if only I had died in your place! O Absalom my son, my son!"

2 Samuel 18:31–33

For a mere moment I have forsaken you,
    But with great mercies I will gather you. . . .
All your children shall be taught by the LORD,
    And great shall be the peace of your children.
                                        Isaiah 54:7, 13

All we like sheep have gone astray;
    We have turned, every one, to his own way;
    And the LORD has laid on Him the iniquity of
        us all.

                                        Isaiah 53:6

For the LORD will not cast off His people,
    Nor will He forsake His inheritance.
But judgment will return to righteousness,
    And all the upright in heart will follow it.
                                        Psalm 94:14–15

So the ransomed of the LORD shall return,
    And come to Zion with singing,
    With everlasting joy on their heads.
    They shall obtain joy and gladness;
    Sorrow and sighing shall flee away.

                                        Isaiah 51:11

"I will not leave you orphans; I will come to you."
                                        John 14:18

You ask for His patience

Fathers, do not provoke your children, lest they become discouraged.

Colossians 3:21

Blessed is he who waits.

Daniel 12:12

The end of a thing is better than its beginning;
   The patient in spirit is better than the proud in
      spirit.

Ecclesiastes 7:8

My brethren, count it all joy when you fall into various trials, knowing that the testing of your faith produces patience. But let patience have its perfect work, that you may be perfect and complete, lacking nothing.

James 1:2–4

Now we exhort you, brethren, warn those who are unruly, comfort the fainthearted, uphold the weak, be patient with all.

1 Thessalonians 5:14

And a servant of the Lord must not quarrel but be gentle to all, able to teach, patient.

2 Timothy 2:24

Therefore we also, since we are surrounded by so great a cloud of witnesses, let us lay aside every weight, and the sin which so easily ensnares us, and let us run with endurance the race that is set before us.

Hebrews 12:1

For even Christ did not please Himself; but as it is written, "The reproaches of those who reproached You fell on Me." For whatever things were written before were written for our learning, that we through the patience and comfort of the Scriptures might have hope. Now may the God of patience and comfort grant you to be like-minded toward one another, according to Christ Jesus.

Romans 15:3–5

And not only that, but we also glory in tribulations, knowing that tribulation produces perseverance.

Romans 5:3

Therefore if there is any consolation in Christ, if any comfort of love, if any fellowship of the Spirit, if any affection and mercy, fulfill my joy by being likeminded, having the same love, being of one accord, of one mind. Let nothing be done through selfish ambition or conceit, but in lowliness of mind let each esteem others better than himself. Let each of you look out not only for his own interests, but also for the interests of others.

Philippians 2:1–4

You ask for His Spirit's guidance

What then shall we say to these things? If God is for us, who can be against us? He who did not spare His own Son, but delivered Him up for us all, how shall He not with Him also freely give us all things?

Romans 8:31–32

Teach me to do Your will,
 For You are my God;
 Your Spirit is good.
 Lead me in the land of uprightness.
Revive me, O Lord, for Your name's sake!
 For Your righteousness' sake bring my soul out
  of trouble.

Psalm 143:10–11

Now the Lord is the Spirit; and where the Spirit of the Lord is, there is liberty. But we all, with unveiled face, beholding as in a mirror the glory of the Lord, are being transformed into the same image from glory to glory, just as by the Spirit of the Lord.

2 Corinthians 3:17–18

For He shall give His angels charge over you,
  To keep you in all your ways.
In their hands they shall bear you up,
  Lest you dash your foot against a stone.
You shall tread upon the lion and the cobra,
  The young lion and the serpent you shall
    trample underfoot.
"Because he has set his love upon Me, therefore I
    will deliver him;
  I will set him on high, because he has known
    My name.
He shall call upon Me, and I will answer him;
  I will be with him in trouble;
  I will deliver him and honor him.
With long life I will satisfy him,
  And show him My salvation."

Psalm 91:11–16

By this we know that we abide in Him, and He in us, because He has given us of His Spirit.

1 John 4:13

For we through the Spirit eagerly wait for the hope of righteousness by faith.

Galatians 5:5

I say then: Walk in the Spirit, and you shall not fulfill the lust of the flesh. For the flesh lusts against the Spirit, and the Spirit against the flesh; and these are contrary to one another, so that you do not do the things that you wish. But if you are led by the Spirit, you are not under the law.

Now the works of the flesh are evident, which are: adultery, fornication, uncleanness, lewdness, idolatry, sorcery, hatred, contentions, jealousies, outbursts of wrath, selfish ambitions, dissensions, heresies, envy, murders, drunkenness, revelries, and the like; of which I tell you beforehand, just as I also told you in time past, that those who practice such things will not inherit the kingdom of God.

But the fruit of the Spirit is love, joy, peace, long-suffering, kindness, goodness, faithfulness, gentleness, self-control. Against such there is no law.

And those who are Christ's have crucified the flesh with its passions and desires. If we live in the Spirit, let us also walk in the Spirit. Let us not become conceited, provoking one another, envying one another.

Galatians 5:16–26

But God has revealed them to us through His Spirit. For the Spirit searches all things, yes, the deep things of God. For what man knows the things of a man except the spirit of the man which is in him? Even so no one knows the things of God except the Spirit of God. Now we have received, not the spirit of the world, but the Spirit who is from God, that we might know the things that have been freely given to us by God.

These things we also speak, not in words which man's wisdom teaches but which the Holy Spirit teaches, comparing spiritual things with spiritual. But the natural man does not receive the things of the Spirit of God, for they are foolishness to him; nor can he know them, because they are spiritually discerned.

But he who is spiritual judges all things, yet he himself is rightly judged by no one. For "who has known the mind of the LORD that he may instruct Him?" But we have the mind of Christ.

1 Corinthians 2:10–16

You admit your shortcomings as a father

O God, do not be far from me;
    O my God, make haste to help me! . . .
My mouth shall tell of Your righteousness
    And Your salvation all the day,
    For I do not know their limits.
I will go in the strength of the Lord GOD;
    I will make mention of Your righteousness, of
        Yours only.
O God, You have taught me from my youth;
    And to this day I declare Your wondrous works.
Now also when I am old and grayheaded,
    O God, do not forsake me,
    Until I declare Your strength to this generation,
    Your power to everyone who is to come.

Psalm 71:12, 15–18

Be of good courage,
    And He shall strengthen your heart,
    All you who hope in the LORD.

Psalm 31:24

For I will pour water on him who is thirsty,
 And floods on the dry ground;
 I will pour My Spirit on your descendants,
 And My blessing on your offspring;
They will spring up among the grass
 Like willows by the watercourses.

Isaiah 44:3–4

Only take heed to yourself, and diligently keep yourself, lest you forget the things your eyes have seen, and lest they depart from your heart all the days of your life. And teach them to your children and your grandchildren.

Deuteronomy 4:9

Now it shall come to pass, if you diligently obey the voice of the LORD your God, to observe carefully all His commandments which I command you today, that the LORD your God will set you high above all nations of the earth. . . .

Blessed shall be the fruit of your body, the produce of your ground and the increase of your herds, the increase of your cattle and the offspring of your flocks.

Deuteronomy 28:1, 4

He who covers his sins will not prosper,
But whoever confesses and forsakes them will
have mercy.

Proverbs 28:13

The LORD is good,
A stronghold in the day of trouble;
And He knows those who trust in Him.

Nahum 1:7

"For how can this servant of my lord talk with you, my lord? As for me, no strength remains in me now, nor is any breath left in me."

Then again, the one having the likeness of a man touched me and strengthened me. And he said, "O man greatly beloved, fear not! Peace be to you; be strong, yes, be strong!"

So when he spoke to me I was strengthened, and said, "Let my lord speak, for you have strengthened me."

Then he said, "Do you know why I have come to you? And now I must return to fight with the prince of Persia; and when I have gone forth, indeed the prince of Greece will come. But I will tell you what is noted in the Scripture of Truth. (No one upholds me against these, except Michael your prince.)"

Daniel 10:17–21

So then neither he who plants is anything, nor he who waters, but God who gives the increase. Now he who plants and he who waters are one, and each one will receive his own reward according to his own labor.

For we are God's fellow workers; you are God's field, you are God's building.

1 Corinthians 3:7–9

Call to Me, and I will answer you, and show you great and mighty things, which you do not know.

Jeremiah 33:3

The LORD is far from the wicked,
But He hears the prayer of the righteous.
The light of the eyes rejoices the heart,
And a good report makes the bones healthy.
The ear that hears the rebukes of life
Will abide among the wise.
He who disdains instruction despises his own soul,
But he who heeds rebuke gets understanding.
The fear of the LORD is the instruction of wisdom,
And before honor is humility.

Proverbs 15:29–33

You're overwhelmed by your family responsibilities

Unless the LORD builds the house,
    They labor in vain who build it;
    Unless the LORD guards the city,
    The watchman stays awake in vain.
It is vain for you to rise up early,
    To sit up late,
    To eat the bread of sorrows;
    For so He gives His beloved sleep.
Behold, children are a heritage from the LORD,
    The fruit of the womb is a reward.
Like arrows in the hand of a warrior,
    So are the children of one's youth.
Happy is the man who has his quiver full of them;
    They shall not be ashamed,
    But shall speak with their enemies in the gate.

Psalm 127:1–5

He gives power to the weak,
    And to those who have no might He increases
      strength.

Isaiah 40:29

"For the mountains shall depart
    And the hills be removed,
    But My kindness shall not depart from you,
    Nor shall My covenant of peace be removed,"
        Says the LORD, who has mercy on you.

Isaiah 54:10

I cried out to God with my voice—
    To God with my voice;
    And He gave ear to me.
I remembered God, and was troubled;
    I complained, and my spirit was overwhelmed.
        Selah.

Psalm 77:1, 3

Fear not, for I am with you;
    I will bring your descendants from the east,
    And gather you from the west;
I will say to the north, "Give them up!"
    And to the south, "Do not keep them back!"
    Bring My sons from afar,
    And My daughters from the ends of the earth—
Everyone who is called by My name,
    Whom I have created for My glory;
    I have formed him, yes, I have made him.

Isaiah 43:5–7

Lift up your eyes on high,
And see who has created these things,
Who brings out their host by number;
He calls them all by name,
By the greatness of His might
And the strength of His power;
Not one is missing.

Isaiah 40:26

Trust in the LORD with all your heart,
And lean not on your own understanding;
In all your ways acknowledge Him,
And He shall direct your paths.
Do not be wise in your own eyes;
Fear the LORD and depart from evil.

Proverbs 3:5–7

When you pass through the waters, I will be
with you;
And through the rivers, they shall not
overflow you.
When you walk through the fire, you shall not
be burned,
Nor shall the flame scorch you.

Isaiah 43:2

Be strong and of good courage, do not fear nor be afraid of them; for the LORD your God, He is the One who goes with you. He will not leave you nor forsake you.

Deuteronomy 31:6

Therefore, brethren, stand fast and hold the traditions which you were taught, whether by word or our epistle.

Now may our Lord Jesus Christ Himself, and our God and Father, who has loved us and given us everlasting consolation and good hope by grace, comfort your hearts and establish you in every good word and work.

2 Thessalonians 2:15–17

GOD COMFORTS
YOU WHEN . . .

You feel inadequate in rearing your children

For the Lord GOD will help Me;
    Therefore I will not be disgraced;
    Therefore I have set My face like a flint,
    And I know that I will not be ashamed.

Isaiah 50:7

But You are the same,
    And Your years will have no end.
The children of Your servants will continue,
    And their descendants will be established
        before You.

Psalm 102:27–28

For the eyes of the LORD run to and fro throughout the whole earth, to show Himself strong on behalf of those whose heart is loyal to Him.

2 Chronicles 16:9

LORD, my heart is not haughty,
    Nor my eyes lofty.
    Neither do I concern myself with great matters,
    Nor with things too profound for me.
Surely I have calmed and quieted my soul,
    Like a weaned child with his mother;
    Like a weaned child is my soul within me.
O Israel, hope in the LORD
    From this time forth and forever.

Psalm 131:1–3

For who makes you differ from another? And what do you have that you did not receive? Now if you did indeed receive it, why do you boast as if you had not received it?

1 Corinthians 4:7

But by the grace of God I am what I am, and His grace toward me was not in vain; but I labored more abundantly than they all, yet not I, but the grace of God which was with me.

1 Corinthians 15:10

Not that we are sufficient of ourselves to think of anything as being from ourselves, but our sufficiency is from God.

2 Corinthians 3:5

Do you know the time when the wild mountain
    goats bear young?
  Or can you mark when the deer gives birth?
Can you number the months that they fulfill?
  Or do you know the time when they bear young?
They bow down,
  They bring forth their young,
  They deliver their offspring.

Job 39:1–3

The wings of the ostrich wave proudly,
  But are her wings and pinions like the kindly
    stork's?
For she leaves her eggs on the ground,
  And warms them in the dust;
She forgets that a foot may crush them,
  Or that a wild beast may break them.
She treats her young harshly, as though they were
    not hers;
  Her labor is in vain, without concern,
Because God deprived her of wisdom,
  And did not endow her with understanding.

Job 39:13–17

By which have been given to us exceedingly great and precious promises, that through these you may be partakers of the divine nature, having escaped the corruption that is in the world through lust.

But also for this very reason, giving all diligence, add to your faith virtue, to virtue knowledge, to knowledge self-control, to self-control perseverance, to perseverance godliness, to godliness brotherly kindness, and to brotherly kindness love. For if these things are yours and abound, you will be neither barren nor unfruitful in the knowledge of our Lord Jesus Christ.

2 Peter 1:4–8

I have blotted out, like a thick cloud, your
    transgressions,
    And like a cloud, your sins.
    Return to Me, for I have redeemed you.
Isaiah 44:22

But we were gentle among you, just as a nursing mother cherishes her own children. So, affectionately longing for you, we were well pleased to impart to you not only the gospel of God, but also our own lives, because you had become dear to us.

1 Thessalonians 2:7–8

I can do all things through Christ who strengthens me.

Philippians 4:13

"Come to Me, all you who labor and are heavy laden, and I will give you rest. Take My yoke upon you and learn from Me, for I am gentle and lowly in heart, and you will find rest for your souls. For My yoke is easy and My burden is light."

Matthew 11:28–30

Your child is seriously ill

Beloved, I pray that you may prosper in all things and be in health, just as your soul prospers.

3 John 2

While He spoke these things to them, behold, a ruler came and worshiped Him, saying, "My daughter has just died, but come and lay Your hand on her and she will live." So Jesus arose and followed him, and so did His disciples. . . .

When Jesus came into the ruler's house, and saw the flute players and the noisy crowd wailing, He said to them, "Make room, for the girl is not dead, but sleeping." And they ridiculed Him. But when the crowd was put outside, He went in and took her by the hand, and the girl arose. And the report of this went out into all that land.

Matthew 9:18–19, 23–26

As one whom his mother comforts,
So I will comfort you;
And you shall be comforted in Jerusalem.

Isaiah 66:13

Then one of the crowd answered and said, "Teacher, I brought You my son, who has a mute spirit. And wherever it seizes him, it throws him down; he foams at the mouth, gnashes his teeth, and becomes rigid. So I spoke to Your disciples, that they should cast it out, but they could not."

He answered him and said, "O faithless generation, how long shall I be with you? How long shall I bear with you? Bring him to Me." Then they brought him to Him. And when he saw Him, immediately the spirit convulsed him, and he fell on the ground and wallowed, foaming at the mouth.

So He asked his father, "How long has this been happening to him?"

And he said, "From childhood. And often he has thrown him both into the fire and into the water to destroy him. But if You can do anything, have compassion on us and help us."

Jesus said to him, "If you can believe, all things are possible to him who believes."

Immediately the father of the child cried out and said with tears, "Lord, I believe; help my unbelief!"

Mark 9:17–24

Now when Jesus had entered Capernaum, a centurion came to Him, pleading with Him, saying, "Lord, my servant is lying at home paralyzed, dreadfully tormented."

And Jesus said to him, "I will come and heal him."

The centurion answered and said, "Lord, I am not worthy that You should come under my roof. But only speak a word, and my servant will be healed. "For I also am a man under authority, having soldiers under me. And I say to this one, 'Go,' and he goes; and to another, 'Come,' and he comes; and to my servant, 'Do this,' and he does it."

When Jesus heard it, He marveled, and said to those who followed, "Assuredly, I say to you, I have not found such great faith, not even in Israel! "And I say to you that many will come from east and west, and sit down with Abraham, Isaac, and Jacob in the kingdom of heaven. But the sons of the kingdom will be cast out into outer darkness. There will be weeping and gnashing of teeth." Then Jesus said to the centurion, "Go your way; and as you have believed, so let it be done for you." And his servant was healed that same hour.

Matthew 8:5–13

Then Nathan departed to his house.

And the LORD struck the child that Uriah's wife bore to David, and it became ill. David therefore pleaded with God for the child, and David fasted and went in and lay all night on the ground. So the elders of his house arose and went to him, to raise him up from the ground. But he would not, nor did he eat food with them. Then on the seventh day it came to pass that the child died. And the servants of David were afraid to tell him that the child was dead. For they said, "Indeed, while the child was alive, we spoke to him, and he would not heed our voice. How can we tell him that the child is dead? He may do some harm!"

When David saw that his servants were whispering, David perceived that the child was dead. Therefore David said to his servants, "Is the child dead?" And they said, "He is dead."

So David arose from the ground, washed and anointed himself, and changed his clothes; and he went into the house of the LORD and worshiped. Then he went to his own house; and when he requested, they set food before him, and he ate. Then his servants said to him, "What is this that you have done? You fasted and wept for the child while he was alive, but when the child died, you arose and ate food."

And he said, "While the child was alive, I fasted and wept; for I said, 'Who can tell whether the LORD will be gracious to me, that the child may live?' But now he is dead; why should I fast? Can I bring him back again? I shall go to him, but he shall not return to me."

Then David comforted Bathsheba his wife, and went in to her and lay with her. So she bore a son, and he called his name Solomon. Now the LORD loved him.

2 Samuel 12:15–24

Is anyone among you sick? Let him call for the elders of the church, and let them pray over him, anointing him with oil in the name of the Lord. And the prayer of faith will save the sick, and the Lord will raise him up. And if he has committed sins, he will be forgiven. Confess your trespasses to one another, and pray for one another, that you may be healed. The effective, fervent prayer of a righteous man avails much.

James 5:14–16

Your wife doesn't seem to understand you

Husbands, likewise, dwell with them with understanding, giving honor to the wife, as to the weaker vessel, and as being heirs together of the grace of life, that your prayers may not be hindered.

Finally, all of you be of one mind, having compassion for one another; love as brothers, be tenderhearted, be courteous; not returning evil for evil or reviling for reviling, but on the contrary blessing, knowing that you were called to this, that you may inherit a blessing. For

"He who would love life
And see good days,
Let him refrain his tongue from evil,
And his lips from speaking deceit.
Let him turn away from evil and do good;
Let him seek peace and pursue it."

1 Peter 3:7–11

For none of us lives to himself, and no one dies to himself.

Romans 14:7

And the Lord God said, "It is not good that man should be alone; I will make him a helper comparable to him." . . .

So Adam gave names to all cattle, to the birds of the air, and to every beast of the field. But for Adam there was not found a helper comparable to him.

And the Lord God caused a deep sleep to fall on Adam, and he slept; and He took one of his ribs, and closed up the flesh in its place. Then the rib which the Lord God had taken from man He made into a woman, and He brought her to the man.

And Adam said:

"This is now bone of my bones
And flesh of my flesh;
She shall be called Woman,
Because she was taken out of Man."

Therefore a man shall leave his father and mother and be joined to his wife, and they shall become one flesh.

And they were both naked, the man and his wife, and were not ashamed.

Genesis 2:18, 20–25

Like a bird that wanders from its nest
Is a man who wanders from his place.

Proverbs 27:8

Though I speak with the tongues of men and of angels, but have not love, I have become sounding brass or a clanging cymbal. And though I have the gift of prophecy, and understand all mysteries and all knowledge, and though I have all faith, so that I could remove mountains, but have not love, I am nothing And though I bestow all my goods to feed the poor, and though I give my body to be burned, but have not love, it profits me nothing.

Love suffers long and is kind; love does not envy; love does not parade itself, is not puffed up; does not behave rudely, does not seek its own, is not provoked, thinks no evil; does not rejoice in iniquity, but rejoices in the truth; Bears all things, believes all things, hopes all things, endures all things.

Love never fails. But whether there are prophecies, they will fail; whether there are tongues, they will cease; whether there is knowledge, it will vanish away.

For we know in part and we prophesy in part. But when that which is perfect has come, then that which is in part will be done away.

When I was a child, I spoke as a child, I understood as a child, I thought as a child; but when I became a man, I put away childish things. For now we see in a mirror, dimly, but then face to face. Now I know in part, but then I shall know just as I also am known.

And now abide faith, hope, love, these three; but the greatest of these is love.

1 Corinthians 13:1–13

A word fitly spoken is like apples of gold
    In settings of silver. . . .
By long forbearance a ruler is persuaded,
    And a gentle tongue breaks a bone.

Proverbs 25:11, 15

Let love be without hypocrisy. Abhor what is evil. Cling to what is good. Be kindly affectionate to one another with brotherly love, in honor giving preference to one another.

Romans 12:9–10

Nevertheless, neither is man independent of woman, nor woman independent of man, in the Lord.

For as woman came from man, even so man also comes through woman; but all things are from God.

1 Corinthians 11:11–12

Two are better than one,
    Because they have a good reward for their labor.
For if they fall, one will lift up his companion.
    But woe to him who is alone when he falls,
    For he has no one to help him up.
Again, if two lie down together, they will keep
      warm;
    But how can one be warm alone?

Ecclesiastes 4:9–11

"For if you love those who love you, what reward have you? Do not even the tax collectors do the same? And if you greet your brethren only, what do you do more than others? Do not even the tax collectors do so? Therefore you shall be perfect, just as your Father in heaven is perfect."

Matthew 5:46–48

Owe no one anything except to love one another, for he who loves another has fulfilled the law. For the commandments, "You shall not commit adultery," "You shall not murder," "You shall not steal," "You shall not bear false witness," "You shall not covet," and if there is any other commandment, are all summed up in this saying, namely, "You shall love your neighbor as yourself." Love does no harm to a neighbor; therefore love is the fulfillment of the law.

Romans 13:8–10

You must discipline your children

My son, do not despise the chastening of the
LORD,
  Nor detest His correction;
For whom the LORD loves He corrects,
  Just as a father the son in whom he delights.

Proverbs 3:11–12

Furthermore, we have had human fathers who corrected us, and we paid them respect. Shall we not much more readily be in subjection to the Father of spirits and live? For they indeed for a few days chastened us as seemed best to them, but He for our profit, that we may be partakers of His holiness. Now no chastening seems to be joyful for the present, but painful; nevertheless, afterward it yields the peaceable fruit of righteousness to those who have been trained by it.

Hebrews 12:9–11

The rod and rebuke give wisdom,
   But a child left to himself brings shame to
      his mother. . . .
Correct your son, and he will give you rest;
   Yes, he will give delight to your soul.

Proverbs 29:15, 17

Though He was a Son, yet He learned obedience by the things which He suffered.

Hebrews 5:8

Now I rejoice, not that you were made sorry, but that your sorrow led to repentance. For you were made sorry in a godly manner, that you might suffer loss from us in nothing.

2 Corinthians 7:9

Chasten your son while there is hope,
   And do not set your heart on his destruction.

Proverbs 19:18

Rebuke is more effective for a wise man
   Than a hundred blows on a fool.

Proverbs 17:10

Hatred stirs up strife,
But love covers all sins.
Wisdom is found on the lips of him who has
understanding,
But a rod is for the back of him who is devoid
of understanding.

Proverbs 10:12–13

Whoever loves instruction loves knowledge,
But he who hates correction is stupid.
A good man obtains favor from the LORD,
But a man of wicked intentions He will
condemn.
A man is not established by wickedness,
But the root of the righteous cannot be moved.

Proverbs 12:1–3

Consecrate yourselves therefore, and be holy, for I
am the LORD your God.

Leviticus 20:7

Therefore be very courageous to keep and to do all
that is written in the Book of the Law of Moses, lest you
turn aside from it to the right hand or to the left. . . .

But you shall hold fast to the LORD your God, as
you have done to this day.

Joshua 23:6, 8

My son, keep my words,
    And treasure my commands within you.
Keep my commands and live,
    And my law as the apple of your eye.
Bind them on your fingers;
    Write them on the tablet of your heart.

Proverbs 7:1–3

You feel powerless to shield your children from evils like drugs and alcohol

Hear, O heavens, and give ear, O earth!
   For the LORD has spoken:
   "I have nourished and brought up children,
   And they have rebelled against Me."

Isaiah 1:2

In the fear of the LORD there is strong confidence,
   And His children will have a place of refuge.
The fear of the LORD is a fountain of life,
   To turn one away from the snares of death.

Proverbs 14:26–27

In the way of righteousness is life,
   And in its pathway there is no death.

Proverbs 12:28

A foolish son is a grief to his father,
   And bitterness to her who bore him.

Proverbs 17:25

Therefore hear me now, my children,
  And do not depart from the words of my
      mouth. . . .
Lest aliens be filled with your wealth,
  And your labors go to the house of a foreigner;
And you mourn at last,
  When your flesh and your body are consumed,
And say:
  "How I have hated instruction,
  And my heart despised correction!
I have not obeyed the voice of my teachers,
  Nor inclined my ear to those who instructed
      me!
I was on the verge of total ruin,
  In the midst of the assembly and congregation."
                              Proverbs 5:7, 10–14

Wine is a mocker,
  Strong drink is a brawler,
  And whoever is led astray by it is not wise.
                              Proverbs 20:1

He who loves pleasure will be a poor man;
  He who loves wine and oil will not be rich.
                              Proverbs 21:17

In mercy and truth
Atonement is provided for iniquity;
And by the fear of the LORD one departs from
evil.

Proverbs 16:6

Take away the dross from silver,
And it will go to the silversmith for jewelry.

Proverbs 25:4

Do you not know that you are the temple of God and that the Spirit of God dwells in you? If anyone defiles the temple of God, God will destroy him. For the temple of God is holy, which temple you are.

1 Corinthians 3:16–17

My son, if sinners entice you,
Do not consent. . . .
So are the ways of everyone who is greedy for gain;
It takes away the life of its owners.

Proverbs 1:10, 19

"And do not fear those who kill the body but cannot kill the soul. But rather fear Him who is able to destroy both soul and body in hell."

Matthew 10:28

For the law of the Spirit of life in Christ Jesus has made me free from the law of sin and death.

Romans 8:2

My son, if you receive my words,
    And treasure my commands within you,
So that you incline your ear to wisdom,
    And apply your heart to understanding;
Yes, if you cry out for discernment,
    And lift up your voice for understanding,
If you seek her as silver,
    And search for her as for hidden treasures;
Then you will understand the fear of the LORD,
    And find the knowledge of God.
For the LORD gives wisdom;
    From His mouth come knowledge and
        understanding;
He stores up sound wisdom for the upright;
    He is a shield to those who walk uprightly;
He guards the paths of justice,
    And preserves the way of His saints.
Then you will understand righteousness and
        justice,
    Equity and every good path.

Proverbs 2:1–9

But whoever listens to me will dwell safely,
   And will be secure, without fear of evil.
                                    Proverbs 1:33

The merciful man does good for his own soul,
   But he who is cruel troubles his own flesh. . . .
Though they join forces, the wicked will not
      go unpunished;
   But the posterity of the righteous will be
      delivered.
                                    Proverbs 11:17, 21

GOD FILLS YOU
WITH JOY WHEN . . .

Your family gives praises
to the Lord

I will extol You, my God, O King;
    And I will bless Your name forever and ever.
Every day I will bless You,
    And I will praise Your name forever and ever.
Great is the LORD, and greatly to be praised;
    And His greatness is unsearchable.
One generation shall praise Your works to another,
    And shall declare Your mighty acts.

Psalm 145:1–4

Both young men and maidens;
    Old men and children.
Let them praise the name of the LORD,
    For His name alone is exalted;
    His glory is above the earth and heaven.
And He has exalted the horn of His people,
    The praise of all His saints—
    Of the children of Israel,
    A people near to Him.
    Praise the LORD!

Psalm 148:12–14

Praise the LORD!

Praise God in His sanctuary;

Praise Him in His mighty firmament!

Praise Him for His mighty acts;

Praise Him according to His excellent greatness!

Praise Him with the sound of the trumpet;

Praise Him with the lute and harp!

Praise Him with the timbrel and dance;

Praise Him with stringed instruments and flutes!

Praise Him with loud cymbals;

Praise Him with clashing cymbals!

Let everything that has breath praise the LORD.

Praise the LORD!

Psalm 150:1–6

Know that the LORD, He is God;

It is He who has made us, and not we ourselves;

We are His people and the sheep of His pasture.

Enter into His gates with thanksgiving,

And into His courts with praise.

Be thankful to Him, and bless His name.

For the LORD is good;

His mercy is everlasting,

And His truth endures to all generations.

Psalm 100:3–5

This people I have formed for Myself;
   They shall declare My praise.

Isaiah 43:21

I will call upon the LORD, who is worthy to
      be praised;
   So shall I be saved from my enemies.

2 Samuel 22:4

I will sing of the mercies of the LORD forever;
   With my mouth will I make known Your
      faithfulness to all generations.
For I have said, "Mercy shall be built up forever;
   Your faithfulness You shall establish in the
      very heavens.
I have made a covenant with My chosen,
   I have sworn to My servant David:
'Your seed I will establish forever,
   And build up your throne to all generations.'"
      Selah.

Psalm 89:1–4

This will be written for the generation to come,
   That a people yet to be created may praise
      the LORD.

Psalm 102:18

"Sing and rejoice, O daughter of Zion! For behold, I am coming and I will dwell in your midst," says the LORD.

Zechariah 2:10

Nebuchadnezzar the king,
To all peoples, nations, and languages that dwell in all the earth:
Peace be multiplied to you.
I thought it good to declare the signs and wonders that the Most High God has worked for me.
How great are His signs,
And how mighty His wonders!
His kingdom is an everlasting kingdom,
And His dominion is from generation to generation.

Daniel 4:1–3

I thank You and praise You,
    O God of my fathers;
    You have given me wisdom and might,
    And have now made known to me what we
        asked of You,
    For You have made known to us the king's
        demand.

Daniel 2:23

But you are a chosen generation, a royal priesthood, a holy nation, His own special people, that you may proclaim the praises of Him who called you out of darkness into His marvelous light.

1 Peter 2:9

May the LORD give you increase more and more,
    You and your children.
May you be blessed by the LORD,
    Who made heaven and earth.
The heaven, even the heavens, are the LORD's;
    But the earth He has given to the children
        of men.
The dead do not praise the LORD,
    Nor any who go down into silence.
But we will bless the LORD
    From this time forth and forevermore.
    Praise the LORD!

Psalm 115:14–18

Your children grow to love Him

The LORD will establish you as a holy people to Himself, just as He has sworn to you, if you keep the commandments of the LORD your God and walk in His ways. Then all peoples of the earth shall see that you are called by the name of the LORD, and they shall be afraid of you.

Deuteronomy 28:9–10

"You are the salt of the earth; but if the salt loses its flavor, how shall it be seasoned? It is then good for nothing but to be thrown out and trampled underfoot by men.

"You are the light of the world. A city that is set on a hill cannot be hidden. Nor do they light a lamp and put it under a basket, but on a lampstand, and it gives light to all who are in the house. Let your light so shine before men, that they may see your good works and glorify your Father in heaven."

Matthew 5:13–16

I love those who love me,
  And those who seek me diligently will find me.
Proverbs 8:17

And the child Samuel grew in stature, and in favor both with the LORD and men.

1 Samuel 2:26

That Christ may dwell in your hearts through faith; that you, being rooted and grounded in love, may be able to comprehend with all the saints what is the width and length and depth and height—to know the love of Christ which passes knowledge; that you may be filled with all the fullness of God.

Ephesians 3:17–19

"At the same time," says the LORD, "I will be the God of all the families of Israel, and they shall be My people." . . .
  The LORD has appeared of old to me, saying:
    "Yes, I have loved you with an everlasting love;
    Therefore with lovingkindness I have drawn
      you."

Jeremiah 31:1, 3

Knowledge puffs up, but love edifies. And if any-one thinks that he knows anything, he knows nothing yet as he ought to know. But if anyone loves God, this one is known by Him.

1 Corinthians 8:1–3

"'And you shall love the LORD your God with all your heart, with all your soul, with all your mind, and with all your strength.' This is the first command-ment."

Mark 12:30

Grace to you and peace from God our Father and the Lord Jesus Christ.

I thank my God always concerning you for the grace of God which was given to you by Christ Jesus, that you were enriched in everything by Him in all utterance and all knowledge, even as the testimony of Christ was confirmed in you, so that you come short in no gift, eagerly waiting for the revelation of our Lord Jesus Christ, who will also confirm you to the end, that you may be blameless in the day of our Lord Jesus Christ. God is faithful, by whom you were called into the fellowship of His Son, Jesus Christ our Lord.

1 Corinthians 1:3–9